# AUSTRALIAN OPALS
# IN COLOUR

## DEDICATION

To the people of the opal fields in Australia

*Overleaf:* Precious opals. A display of gems demonstrating the wide colour variations of opals from the Australian fields.

# AUSTRALIAN OPALS IN COLOUR

*Nance and Ron Perry* F.G.A.A.

## CHARLES E. TUTTLE COMPANY: PUBLISHERS
*Rutland, Vermont & Tokyo, Japan*

# CONTENTS

This Tuttle edition is the only edition authorized for sale in North America, South America, Middle East, and Asia

Published by the Charles E. Tuttle Company, Inc., of Rutland, Vermont and Tokyo, Japan with editorial offices at Suido 1-chome, 2-6, Bunkyo-ku, Tokyo, Japan by special arrangement with A. H. & A. W. Reed, Wellington, Auckland, and Sydney. © 1969 by N. and R. Perry. All rights reserved. Library of Congress Catalog Card No. 72-109413. Standard Book No. 8048 0862-7. Printed in Japan.

# PREFACE

THE beauty and fascination of an opal of gem quality lie in the depth and variety of its colours. Opals have been admired and studied for generations, but the many attempts to understand the reasons for the colours have been unsuccessful until quite recently. Australia is now the main producer of gem-quality opals, and it is therefore particularly gratifying that the discovery of the structure of the material and the explanation of the origin of its colour were made by Australian scientists working in the laboratories of the CSIRO.

A close study of good-quality gem opals shows that they consist of patches or grains; the colour is generally uniform within each grain, but varies from grain to grain. If the gemstone is tilted around, all of the colours will change. We call this the "play of colour" and it is this property of ever-changing colours which gives opals their distinctive attraction, and which has been so hard to understand.

There are a number of quite different physical principles involved in the colours of various types of gemstones. In the simplest cases, gems such as ruby, sapphire, emerald, etc. owe their body colours to the absorption of some wavelengths of light by small amounts of impurities, without which these substances would be quite colourless, like window-glass. The coloured flash of diamonds and brilliants comes from dispersion of light by *refraction*, because different colours are bent at different angles when white light passes through the surface between air and the gem. The colours in opals are now known to be produced by an entirely different phenomenon called *diffraction*, where white light is split into its spectral colours within the gem. This occurs because each grain in the opal consists of a regular arrangement of silica particles, whose diameter is about equal to the wavelength of visible light. The colours in the play of opal always follow the order of the colours in the spectrum and obey the scientific laws of diffraction. How this happens has already been described in the Perry's previous book, *Australian Gemstones in Colour*.

These changing colours in the play of opals are very difficult to capture in photographs. In fact some people who have tried to photograph the colours have been so unsuccessful that they have concluded that it is impossible, and this elusive property has added to the mystery of the gemstone. The Perrys have overcome this difficulty and their results appear here as a successful series of colour plates of many types of opal.

One of the fascinations of opal is the great variety of forms it takes. The appearance depends upon the size, orientation and structure of the grains, which may be very small, as in pin-fire opal, or large enough to fill a whole stone, when a single band of colour will roll across the gem as it is tilted. Many of these different types can be seen here in the photographs.

Once it was realised that precious opals consisted of ordered arrangements of small silica particles, some thought was given to the possibility of producing synthetic opals, and experiments were initiated in CSIRO laboratories. The experiments showed that it was possible to make silica spheres of sufficient size and uniformity, and to organise them into the regular arrays necessary for the production of colour. The product was of poor quality by comparison with the natural material, and present experiments are aimed at improving the hardness and transparency of the synthetic gem. In order to protect Australian interests, a patent application was made in 1964 on the basis of this process.

We know that this book will be read avidly by many already familiar with opals, from those who gouge underground to those who cut and polish and sell the gems. In addition it will be read by others who have not yet been caught with the opal bug, and we hope that it will inspire them to join this growing band, for whom opals outshine all other gems.

P. J. DARRAGH
*CSIRO Division of Applied Mineralogy*

J. V. SANDERS
*CSIRO Division of Tribophysics*

# INTRODUCTION

OPAL, the gem of flashing spectrum colours, is "big business" in Australia today.

Values have leapt upwards in the last two years, as buyers from the East, United States, Germany, Austria and the Netherlands show increasing interest in both rough and cut stones. The value of opal exported from Australia has reached the annual figure of $8,000,000

Precious opal has been taken from five main areas: White Cliffs and Lightning Ridge in NSW, Coober Pedy, and Andamooka in South Australia, and the scattered fields in Queensland. Opal from Queensland accounts for a very small percentage of the yield. Today Coober Pedy and Andamooka are the main producers of the world's opal.

Not all opal is colourful, and only the opal with colour is "precious". It does not occur in great quantities. It is shy of discovery and hard to win.

"But there must be lots of it—somewhere," the oldtimers say wistfully. "It's only a matter of time before somebody strikes it again, and then there'll be another rush."

The "opal game" is a game of chance, and chance has always attended its discovery. A few pretty pebbles (floaters) lying on the surface of the earth are usually the first tell-tale signs of its presence underground.

In tracing the history of the recovery of Australian opal difficulty is found in sifting fact from fancies, and truth from legends. Dates have been forgotten, values exaggerated or understated, positions of finds have been confused. And the official and true value of all the opal found will *never* be recorded.

Opal is a gem of power, a tantalising gem. It is a "Gem of a Thousand Lights". It imprisons colours which have spanned millions of centuries. Every man becomes a poet when he looks upon an opal. It is a primaeval gem, prehistoric, ancient and unique. It is the Rainbow Rock for which many people brave many hardships.

Opal was old before man was born. It had been in existence for sixty million years before man emerged from the mists of time: yet it is still being formed. It is a link with many yesterdays. Shells and the bones of prehistoric animals have been found completely replaced by precious opal.

No other precious stone can be compared with

it. Peacock colours glow and throb, and pulse and vibrate as the stone is turned. They dart from the stone. Deep down, latent colours wait for the correct angle of light to bring them leaping to the surface.

Opal had been known to occur in Australia since the mid-nineteenth century, but no great significance was attached to its discovery. It was worked in Queensland in the 1870s, but it was not until kangaroo-hunters found opal in 1889 about 140 miles north-east of Broken Hill that the first big rush began, at White Cliffs in NSW.

Opal-mining at White Cliffs was weary work, with little return for most miners. A shanty town sprang up rapidly. A Cobb & Co coach service was provided for buyers. As on most gem fields in this hot and thirsty country, the hotel did the best trade of all.

The white sandstone yielded opal for the lucky ones over a period of fifteen years before it was pronounced played-out.

Although the brilliant black opal had been found at Lightning Ridge in the 1880s, it was not recognised as valuable, nor appreciated as a rare gem. Mining did not begin there in earnest until about 1902. Knowing the value of black opal today, it is incredible to realise that the first attempts to market it were disappointing and unsuccessful.

But "Fashion" fell in love with Australian opal, and soon it was in demand. Miners flocked to the field at Lightning Ridge, and their shafts and mullock heaps changed the landscape to its present crater-like contours.

The superstition that opal brings bad luck is still all too often accepted by people who should know better. They allege that they would not wear the gracious gem for fear of the devil, or worse.

Once a young bride was given a box of opals by her geologist husband on his return from a field trip. "I couldn't get them out of the house quickly enough", she confided. "I threw them out with the rubbish—that was twenty years ago—I suppose they might have been quite valuable today."

Another girl was given a bag of opals by a miner who was courting her. She became ill, and a girlfriend who nursed her found the bag with its precious stones—and out they went.

A woman was admiring opals in a jeweller's window in Sydney. She turned to her friend. "Aren't they beautiful!" she exclaimed. "But of course I couldn't possibly wear one. So unlucky." It is said that the big diamond monopolies of past years, seeing the threat in opals, started the "bad luck" legend.

In these enlightened days intelligent people know that if any luck is attached to opal, it can only be good luck—good luck for the miner who finds it, good luck for the economy of the country, and good luck for the person who wears it, and whose jewellery is thereby admired.

The best quality black opal is more expensive than diamonds. It is rare, and of supreme beauty. It is the ultimate in gem loveliness.

Colour in opal may occur in giant flakes, and change from green to orange, and from red to blue as the stone is turned. Or the colour may occur in patterns which resemble landscapes or objects. Harlequin flash (like a checkerboard) and pinfire opal (with many scintillating points) with predominant reds are the two which are most eagerly sought.

The colour in a high value opal should not be clouded, or interrupted by potch or sand. There should be no cracks, scores, or crazes in the stone. A black opal about the size of a dried pea could be valued at $100. Gem quality Lightning Ridge opal brings upwards of $100 per carat, or $3,000 per troy ounce.

Opal has earned more income for the state of NSW than any other gem. This much is positively known, even though obvious difficulties prevent anything more than an official estimate.

The value of opals is assessed on colour. A small but exquisitely coloured stone will carry more value than a larger stone which lacks fire and/or carries a mist of potch. Colours must be clear and vibrant.

Stones which show all colours of the spectrum, or at least the four primary colours (red, blue, green and yellow), and do not lose their colour when turned in a full circle are most highly prized. Stones in which "the light does not go out" are sought in preference to stones which show their brightest colours from one or two directions only.

Many extremely beautiful stones, however, have the property of showing bright colours from only one or two directions. It is the element of brilliant colour-surprise as the opal is viewed from changing angles that attracts most people and enhances their appreciation of the stone.

Solid black opals from Lightning Ridge top the scale of values. Then follow lighter Lightning Ridge solids, clear opal from Queensland, and Andamooka and Coober Pedy solids.

Opal doublets and triplets sell for as much as $500 if large and showy enough. Souvenir and small white stones and doublets may be bought for as low as $2.00. Pairs and sets in both solids and doublets carry a 15 per cent to 50 per cent premium.

Opal deals on the field, with due consideration given to the value of money spent, are conducted with amazing simplicity. Transactions for enormous sums take place in the hotel bar, a hut, or a dugout, or in the local café over steak and eggs. Both parties wear shorts (and a shirt too if ladies are present). Their feet may be comfortably bare. It is a thirsty country, and beer or wine carry the deal to a mutually satisfactory conclusion. There are no written contracts. Just cash.

Stones of great value are carried in cigarette tins, or small plastic boxes. Rough opal is stored and sold in gelignite bags.

There are no fixed prices for the various types and grades of rough opal. Parcels on the field sell by the law of supply and demand. If a miner has a good backing, and is in no hurry for money, he can afford to hold to his price.

If he needs cash to pay his account at the store, or buy a new "jalopy" or take a trip south, he will sell his opal more cheaply. Before Christmas on some of the fields amazing bargains are sometimes on offer.

The discerning buyer takes advantage of price fluctuations, with his knowledge of quality and a view to his own market.

Overseas events affect the sale and value of opal. If money is tight, because of war or taxes in the bigger consumer countries, values will ease. But it is generally considered that knowledgable investment in good opal is sound. Opal is a rare commodity. And it is generally conceded that the price will continue to rise.

In farflung fields such as Coober Pedy and Andamooka, the miners are friendly towards the visitor. Many are lonely. Their families may be half a world away in Yugoslavia, Czechoslovakia, Germany, Italy, Sweden, or Greece.

When the Snowy Mountains Authority disbanded many of its work teams, the crews gravitated to the opal fields to try their luck. Many soon became wealthy men. Others continue to work in the hope that each new day will bring their fortune. And it often does. The new Australians love the freedom of the great wide spaces of the inland, where a man is unrestricted, and he can tell an oppressive neighbour sincerely and firmly to go to hell.

Opal, both cut stones and rough material, is mostly sold in "parcels". Each parcel will contain a mixture of qualities, and the discerning buyer will know at a glance whether he will be able to sell at a profit, or, if he is a cutter, whether he will be able to "cut his way out of it". He will separate the various grades into smaller parcels for resale or for cutting.

When cut stones are sold as parcels their number may range from two to ten thousand stones. In retail shops opal solids, doublets and triplets may be bought at the "each" price. When a miner offers a parcel of rough or cut stones, it is the unwritten law that the buyer take the whole parcel—no picking and choosing or taking only the best pieces.

When opal is exported it is often sent to a bank which has been nominated by the proposed purchaser, for his inspection and final decision.

Cut stones and top quality rough are sold by carat weight (155.517 carats in a troy ounce). Lesser grades of rough are sold by troy ounces. Some cutters tend to leave an unnecessary amount of potch on their stones to increase the carat weight, and this is especially noticeable in many black opals. Experienced buyers make allowance for this.

Miners who do not cut stones take their rough to opal cutters. As they work in partnership, when very valuable material is found they both take it along to the cutter, and watch while the stones take shape, to avoid the possibility of any "monkey business".

An odd practice has been for the cutter to place a value on the stones, and charge a percentage for his work on this basis, to be paid when the stones are sold. This could be an unsatisfactory arrangement, as he may be tempted to overvalue the stones to increase his percentage. On the South Australian fields cutters charge a flat rate of a few dollars to cut a stone from poor to moderate quality.

Oddly enough, Australian people do not appear to place much value on the premier gem of their own country. Australia is considered a poor market for gemstones and jewellery, when compared with those overseas. Most large opals find their way to the USA as collectors' pieces.

Opal miners search for beauty. Their greatest grievance is that the best opal is sold to overseas countries. They would like some outstanding specimens to remain in the country of its origin, perhaps to be purchased by governmental or cultural institutions for display to the Australian public, and so preserved for posterity in the land where it was found.

# GLOSSARY

*CARAT*: A measure of weight. 155.517 carats to the troy ounce.

*CONGLOMERATE*: Rock which consists of rounded stones joined together by a cementing substance.

*CRINOID*: Sea-lily from ancient times.

*CRYPTO-CRYSTALLINE*: Tightly packed sub-microscopic crystals.

*DOUBLET*: A two-piece stone.

*DUGOUT*: A house excavated out of a hill—an underground dwelling.

*FERRUGINOUS*: Of the colour of iron.

*GYPSUM*: Hydrous calcium sulphate, hardness 2, occurs massive in sedimentary rocks.

*JALOPY*: Australian slang term of affection for a motor car.

*JASPER*: A variety of quartz.

*JELLY OPAL*: Clear, almost colourless opal.

*KAOLIN*: China clay—a silicate of aluminium.

*MOHS' SCALE*: A scale of hardness used in mineral determination.

*MULGA*: Acacia, or "wattle".

*MULLOCK*: Waste rock and earth produced in mining.

*NAME-STONE*: A stone which warrants the conferment of a name.

*NOBBY*: Opal which has replaced clay nodules.

*NOODLE*: To search for small pieces of opal on mullock heaps.

*OLD-TIMER*: One who has spent the greater number of his years on an opal field.

*ON SPECK*: Unexpectedly.

*PILLAR*: Very little shoring is used in opal mines. When digging the mine, pillars of sandstone are left at intervals to support the ceiling.

*POTCH*: Common opal, usually white, grey or black.

*SANDSTONE*: Grains of fine or coarse sand cemented together.

*SEAM*: Thin infilling of opal in horizontal or vertical fissures.

*SHANTY*: Primitive dwelling.

*SOLID*: A one-piece stone.

*STEELBAND*: Hard sandstone, impregnated with common opal.

*TRIPLET*: A three-piece stone.

*TROY OUNCE*: Equals 1.097136 oz avoir, 480 grains, 20 pennyweights.

*WILLY-WILLY*: Australian term for a small localised duststorm.

# OPAL FIELDS IN AUSTRALIA

THE OPAL AREA in N.W. New South Wales is roughly triangular in shape. Towns in this triangle include Angledool, Cumborah, Collarenebri, Lightning Ridge and Walgett.

This area is covered with black soil plains, broken by low ridges and hills and composed of sediments of probably Cretaceous Age, of not over a hundred feet in height.

Precious opal is found in these sediments.

Mining at Lightning Ridge did not begin until 1904, although opal had been known there for many years before. In those early days, around 1880, black opal was not considered to have any commercial value. The first parcels could not be sold when offered in Sydney and London. In 1904 black opal was eventually sold, and from that time began the climb to dizzy heights of value. Best quality black opal is now more expensive than diamonds. And it is a lot more rare.

There were several rushes to the Lightning Ridge fields, especially to the golden Three Mile. This was a tremendously rich field, and in its heyday clamoured with the influx of over 3,000 miners. The present township of Lightning Ridge is five miles east of this old field.

Rushes also took miners to Bald Hill, in 1915, and to Telephone Line in 1919. In 1926 there was a rush to Grawin, in 1927 to Potch Point, and in 1928 to New Angledool.

One of the most famous opals of all time was found at Angledool—the *Pandora*—4½in × 2½in, and six ounces in weight.

Other localities at Lightning Ridge made famous by fact and by legend are the Nine Mile, Six Mile, Four Mile, Hawks Nest, Frog Hollow, The Flat, Bullock's Head, Nobbys, Dry Rush, Cleared Line, Pony Fence, New Chum, Old Chum, and Sim's Hill.

The following information on the occurence of opal at Lightning Ridge is taken from notes made available by courtesy of the NSW Department of Mines:

Precious opal occurs within the Finch Claystone, usually at or near its junction with the overlying Wallangulla Sandstone and underband which is sometimes formed at this junction. This steelband is a thin (up to one foot layer of hard siliceous sandstone.

Opal either occurs as nodules (known locally as "nobbies") or in seams or thin layers. The nodules are elliptical in shape and some of these have small protuberances on one side to form "tear drops".

Seams are formed along joint planes within the clayshale either horizontally or vertically. In some instances silica has replaced both organic and inorganic material (calcium carbonate from bivalves and crinoid stems, clay nodules, and plant remains), to form opal.

Opal has replaced shells and animal bones.

At one location, Belars, every nobby found was a replaced shell.

## TINTENBAR

TINTENBAR—emerald green curving hills amongst rich dairying country of coastal northern NSW—is in sharp contrast to the red and dry country where precious opal is found on the main Australian fields. In these hills opal was found in volcanic steamholes. It was mainly flawed, and useless except as a curiosity. Stones cut from Tintenbar opal show many cracks, and develop more as time goes on.

Opal has been found also in trachyte at Tooraweenah and Bingara in NSW, but it is too fractured to be of any use, and has been found in steamholes in vesicular lava near the Abercrombie River.

Opalised sandstone has been found at Ballina and Lismore.

Opal sometimes occurs as a filling in steam holes in volcanic rocks. Several such occurrences are known in Australia, but the opal is of no commercial value as the stones are small, badly flawed, and break when cut.

# SOUTH AUSTRALIAN FIELDS

OPAL MINING at Coober Pedy and Andamooka is to shallow depths, rarely exceeding a hundred feet at Coober Pedy and fifty feet at Andamooka. Shafts follow the opal horizon.

On both fields the opal horizon is overlain by siliceous claystone with fibrous gypsum bands, clay and sandstone, often with conglomerate and porcelanite.

At Coober Pedy the precious opal occurs as veinlets or as shells replaced by opal in a ferruginous sandstone.

Although some veins are vertical, they are more generally horizontal. They rarely exceed two inches in thickness.

The value of opal production in South Australia is reputed to reach millions of dollars each year.

# OPAL FROM QUEENSLAND

PROSPECTORS, miners and geologists all concede that the Queensland opal fields are far from worked-out.

The main deterrent to prospecting is lack of water in that part of the country where it is suspected that opal occurs. Brave souls venture out, collect a supply of opal, and return to civilisation to cut or sell it. Even more hardy souls live and work in the lonely outback.

Although in the late 1900s the Queensland fields were actively worked and prosperous, a series of drought years forced people away from the hastily-built towns. The fields are now almost neglected. Common opal is abundant, but precious opal is rare.

Miners from Lightning Ridge drift north to try their luck on the Queensland fields, but the permanent population remains low in number.

The main fields of opal recovery lie in the Yowah, Duck Creek, Quilpie, Eromanga-Windorah, Blackall-Yaraka, Jundah, Opalton, and Kynuna Districts.

The type of opal varies with each area. It may be in ironstone or sandstone matrix, as kernels in siliceous ironstone boulders or "nuts", in seams or "pipes", or as fillings in fractures in sandstone.

Some mines date from the late 1800s and are called by fanciful names, e.g. Quart Pot, The Yellow Nell, Little Wonder, The Aladdin, Hen's Nest, Bung Bung, Exhibition, Breakfast Creek, Aurora Borealis, and Horse Creek.

Peak production occurred in 1895, with opal valued at £32,750.

Western Queensland opal occurs in a 250 mile wide belt, which extends for nearly 600 miles from Kynuna in the north-west to Hungerford in the south.

A series of low, white, flat-topped hills forms low ranges, rarely more than 200 feet high. Beneath these lie the Cretaceous rocks of the Great Artesian Basin. Over the years opal which filtered in as siliceous solutions has been deposited

AUSTRALIAN OPAL FIELDS

QUEENSLAND FIELDS
COOBER PEDY
ANDAMOOKA
LIGHTNING RIDGE
WHITE CLIFFS

AUSTRALIA

Darwin
KIMBERLEY PLATEAU
Anthonys Lagoon
NORTHERN
Cairns
AGATE CREEK
GREAT SANDY DESERT
Tennant Creek
BARKLY TABLELAND
Forsayth
Townsville
Roebourne
Nullagine
Mount Isa
Cloncurry
TERRITORY
QUEENSLAND
Kynuna
Winton
WESTERN
Alice Springs
HARTS RANGE
SIMPSON DESERT
Rockhampton
Anakie
Cue
AUSTRALIA
SOUTH
Quilpie
Charleville
GREAT VICTORIA DESERT
Geraldton
Coober Pedy
AUSTRALIA
Murgon
Toowoomba
BRISBANE
Moora
Kalgoorlie
NULLARBOR
STURT DESERT
Lightning Ridge
NEW ENGLAND DIST
Stanthorpe
Andamooka
White Cliffs
Tamworth
PERTH
NEW
Broken Hill
SOUTH WALES
Pemberton
Albany
ADELAIDE
Bathurst
SYDNEY
CANBERRA
Beechworth
MELBOURNE
VICTORIA

TASMANIA
Launceston
HOBART

as replacements of gypsum, shells, fossils, woody tissue, and it has filled cavities.

Fields in the Cunnamulla District include Yowah, Black Gate, and Elbow, also the Koroit Opal Field, and the Fiery Cross Field.

The Toompine District encompasses the Duck Creek Opal Field, the New Field, the Old Field, Goodman's Flat, the One-mile Workings, Sheep Station Creek, Emu Creek, Pride of the Hills Mine, and the Lushington Mines.

The Bull's Creek Opal Field is in the Quilpie District, also the Marble Arch Mine, the Valdare Mine, and the Hayricks Opal Mine.

Some of the oldest mines in Queensland are in the Eromanga-Windorah District, which is notorious for its shortage of water.

The first discovery of precious opal in Queensland, in 1872, was on Listowel Downs, sixty miles south of Blackall.

On the Jundah Opal Field precious opal occurs in "pipes". These vary from $\frac{1}{8}$in to 3in in diameter, and may be six feet in length. They are roughly cylindrical. They are filled with a hard siliceous, clayey material, coloured by oxide of iron. These brick pipes very probably owe their origin to trunks and portions of trees which have become replaced by opalising solutions and fragments of the enclosing rock.

The Opalton deposit, about seventy miles from Winton, was one of the largest and most extensively worked in Queensland. Opal was first discovered in this district at the Horse Creek Mines, about twenty-five miles south of Opalton, in 1888.

The Kynuna Field is in the Windsor Mining eighteen miles south of the Kynuna township, and is accessible by road from Winton. Prospecting and mining on this field have been generally unsuccessful over the past twenty-five years.

# TYPES OF OPAL MINING

MINING AT ALL FIELDS is usually to shallow depths. Opal may be worked on several levels in a single claim. In one claim at Lightning Ridge opal was found at eleven levels.

Very little mechanisation has so far been used at Lightning Ridge. The South Australian fields have introduced petrol-driven hoists to save labour and time in hauling the opal dirt to the surface. Compressors are commonly used for drilling, and for operating pneumatic shovels. Gelignite is blown at all times of the day or night.

Big D9 caterpillar tractors 'doze away the earth's surface until opal level is reached in huge open cuts. The dirt is powder-fine, and fossickers can sink to their knees in it. Since the dirt is 'dozed up and off the claim, pickings are anybody's gain.

All the necessary basic miners' equipment can be bought on the fields.

At Lightning Ridge the opal occurs in small nodules, or in thin seams along joint planes within the clayshale, or as replacement of shells, crinoid stems and other organic materials.

At Coober Pedy it occurs as either horizontal or vertical bands to two inches thick, and as replacement of shells. Squids' beaks, completely opalised, are not uncommon.

At Andamooka the opal occurs in the interstices of a conglomerate, and as a film on thin layers on boulders. Sometimes it is found as seams within clay under the band of conglomerate which is usually the opal horizon. Opalised skeletons of reptiles have been found—even opalised human bones.

**Plate 2:** Opal from three fields, in three different states of Australia. The opals in the old brooch (*centre*) are examples of solid black opal from Lightning Ridge. It is a quaint fact that some people in Australia today possess uncut opals which they believe to be almost worthless. When black opal was first discovered towards the late 1800s it was scarcely received as a gemstone.

The misconception of the value of opal has persisted right down to the present day. Too often the family black sheep or ne'er-do-well would drift to the opal diggings and bring home a bag of stones for his long-suffering but unappreciative family. Many such gems could lie today forgotten in drawers and cupboards.

The opal in the pendant, (*top left*) and the white stone (*bottom right*) are Coober Pedy opals. The greatest part of the opal produced in Australia comes from Coober Pedy, where mechanical boring machines, bulldozers and compressors are used to remove the sandstone and kaolin to opal level. The very best Coober Pedy opal is not as valuable as Lightning Ridge black opal, but can be comparable with Andamooka opal. Coober Pedy crystal can easily be confused with crystal from Andamooka or Queensland or Lightning Ridge.

Coober Pedy "grey" opal is however, easily recognised. The colour occurs in flakes or flashes in a cream or pale grey potch. It is much less expensive than crystal opal. Large pieces of grey, such as the *Olympic Australis*, become collectors' items.

(*Top right*) A flawless and valuable stone of Queensland opal. To many connoisseurs, Queensland opal is the most brilliant and colourful of all. (*Bottom left*) A small Queensland stone, with unique ironstone markings, suggesting eyebrows.

# VISITING LIGHTNING RIDGE

THE BARWON RIVER is the last river crossed when approaching Lightning Ridge from the south. There is a most remarkable road bridge here. It is a one-way bridge built rather cunningly so that the motorist cannot see whether another vehicle has already started across it from the other side.

When there is water in the river the scene has a picture-postcard quality. In seasons of drought the dry riverbed is but a symbol of all the dry creeks for miles around. In dry seasons the grass withers, and sheep in this country of the black soil plains grow thin and weak. When they die their bones bleach by the side of the road and in the parched paddocks.

Between the Barwon and Lightning Ridge kangaroos and emus roam free. Flocks of pink galahs swoop noisily amongst the trees. Where the trees are only mirages that shimmer in a silver blue lake, the galahs settle in noisy confusion on the stony earth.

Wallangulla was the original name for Lightning Ridge, which is situated within the boundaries of Wallangulla Shire.

A legend, probably born in a slight seed of truth, tells that one night long ago a mob of sheep was struck and killed on the ridge. From then onwards the place was known as Lightning Ridge.

The road between Coonamble and Walgett, almost completely tarred, holds no terrors for motorists these days. But the road between Walgett and Lightning Ridge is not scheduled, according to rumour, to be tarred until 1970. Deep "bull" dust in the dry, or cloggy mud in the wet, tests the skill of drivers, or brings the car to a stop.

Mob of newly shorn sheep near Lightning Ridge.

**Plate 3:** The Barwon River at Walgett.

Lightning Ridge can be reached in one day from Sydney—a 471 mile run—in a reasonable car. Visitors who make a two-day trip of it may stop overnight at Wellington, Dubbo or Coonamble, where comfortable motels or adequate camping grounds are available.

Out from Collarenebri, until the gentle rise up the low hill to Lightning Ridge, the country is red, and lightly timbered with hardy eucalypts. Kangaroos and emus are to be seen. Unhappily, they are attracted by car headlights, and dash into the path of many vehicles. It is a good plan to fit a "kangaroo light" to your car if travelling at night.

The country at Lightning Ridge in its virgin state, was similar to this.

Unlike the South Australian opal fields, Lightning Ridge is truly scenic, without the bald starkness of the "inner inland". It is a

An invitation at Lightning Ridge to view an opal mine without going down a hole.

charming place for a holiday, and you may even return home with enough opal to cover your expenses.

The children will have a wonderful time. Life is free and uninhibited. They can run wild. They need but few clothes—there's no need to dress for dinner in a tent. As long as they are old enough to realise the danger of falling down the mine holes they can have carefree days. And children are very swift to recognise opal.

There is a good camping area at Lightning Ridge, and a town swimming pool, with water from the artesian bore.

The café serves meals, or you can buy your stores at the "cash and carry". Fresh milk is brought in daily from Walgett.

Hotel and motel accommodation at the Ridge is limited to date, so it is wise to book well ahead. Try not to arrive "on spec", or you could be without a bed for the night. The "Tramotel" (trams, of course) has stationary caravans for rent also. Tourist coaches include Lightning Ridge on their Far West itinerary, and always allow some time for a "fossick".

Once the country has been "rushed" for opal, tall white heaps of mullock appear on the surface of the ground. Soon the trees and the grass disappear—they may never return. A glaring, white, lunar landscape takes form. Roads wander from here to there and everywhere. These roads are not too unkind to cars, and some lead out over cattle grids into opal country. A cloud of red dust (or white dust in worked areas) will follow the car. And eventually all roads lead back to the hotel and township.

Easter weekend brings most visitors for the year to Lightning Ridge. Perhaps 3,000. The weather in late March or April has cooled to a pleasant temperature. On Good Friday cars

**Plate 4:** On the road to the opal fields.

**Plate 5:** Below: The lunar landscape of Lightning Ridge.

(many pulling caravans) come by road over the low hill into the white heaps of the opal land. By nightfall a thick mist of red hangs motionless in the hollow down by the hotel.

Infinite space, bright blue skies, timeless days, brilliant sunsets, and velvet black nights, with everyone talking of opal—this is the Ridge.

The outskirts of Lightning Ridge will surprise the visitor who breasts the low ridge for the first time. He finds himself in alien country: instead of flat plains, low eucalypts and a red or black soil, there is just a white mass of undulating heaps stretching as far as the eye can see. These heaps continue over the hill and down almost into the town.

The whole area has been declared a mining reserve, and land allocation is controlled by the Western Lands Commission. Tiny wooden, fibro, or corrugated-iron shacks line the road at intervals. They all offer opals for sale—cut stones, or bottles of chips. It is virtually impossible to buy opal in the rough at Lightning Ridge. Most of the

Part of the "Tramotel" which offers accommodation at Lightning Ridge.

miners have equipped themselves with cutting machinery to work the rare stones themselves.

When you reach the hotel, you have reached the town. At Lightning Ridge the hotel bar is the meeting-place for all the world. Shorts, sandshoes and an old straw hat are quite acceptable dress for a gentleman. Not long ago the following appeal was made in the café as an encouragement to gracious living—"Gents, please wear singlets while dining".

There are four good stores in the town, which supply most of the community's needs—a small department store, a café, a miners' co-operative, and a clothing store. There is also a petrol station.

Water comes up hot from the lower regions. The artesian bore supplies running water to the town, but miners who live a few miles out must get their water in drums. Some housewives take their washing to the bore, and hang it to dry on the nearest tree or fence; sometimes their work is spoiled by clouds of red dust, especially if a car goes past, or a wind rises.

GENTS PLEASE WEAR SINGLETS OR SHIRTS WHILE DINING...

A sign once displayed in a cafe at Lightning Ridge.

**Plate 6:** Digger's Rest Hotel, Lightning Ridge.

**Plate 7:** Main Street, Lightning Ridge.

Entrance to the town of Lightning Ridge.

The miner who owns this dwelling prefers to live upstairs.

Rural electricity serves the town itself but huts and tents on the diggings use hurricane lamps or generators.

Some opal buyers live permanently on the field. Others make regular visits from other parts of Australia or from USA or Japan.

Lightning Ridge is a small community of some 200 people, the township lies 300 miles inland in NSW. It is thirty miles from the Queensland border, and forty-one miles from the nearest town of Walgett.

Houses are small, built of fibro, timber, or concrete block, and are of simple design. There are many huts and caravans on the field. Some huts made of piled stones have survived since the days of the big opal rushes when more than 3,000 miners dug for riches. Such huts have had many owners for, once they strike it rich, very few miners stay on at the Ridge.

An increasing interest in the opal fields by tourists, both local and overseas, has set the stage for changes at Lightning Ridge. Several

**Plate 8:** (*right*) Caravan home and gemstone shop

**Plate 9:** Miner's shack, built about fifty years ago. "Im. provements" include motor tyres to hold up the roof beams, corrugated iron shingles, and aluminium foil wall coverings. Chips of opal nobbies have been found in the walls and chimney, and on the bare ground nearby.

more motels and shops are planned. Crown land building sites in and near the present site, and on the Collarenebri road, have been made available for this purpose at a leasehold rate of $10 per year. Building should begin by the end of the year after allotment.

Life at Lightning Ridge may have the jealousies and feuds usual in any small town or it may be free and easy, but it can never be dull.

The town itself is in a hollow. The Ridge rises suddenly from the flat plain. Tough eucalypts and casuarinas grow wildly in the red sandy soil. Parched grasses struggle to provide a ground cover. Fringes of short trees line the outskirts of

Visitors chat to a miner above his shaft.

high pink and white mullock heaps, which glare and dazzle in the eternal sunlight: mile after mile of white opal dirt, thrown up with infinite toil to form junior mountains of hope and disappointment.

A miner will never tell a visitor "exactly" where to find opal. And you should never ask him *directly*. He may tell you long stories about where it has been found in the past, the weight, the value, the buyers. But you may be sure he will skilfully lead you away from his own favourite location.

However, only about ten square miles at Lightning Ridge have been exploited.

If a miner takes a liking to you, he will invite you into his hut for a cup of tea. He will show you his treasures. Perhaps he has opals which he will sell, and usually he will have some which he will never sell, for it is not uncommon for miners to form an attachment for one or more stones. These, money could never buy: his luck might run out if he sold them. He may be living on the counter lunch at the hotel or on one small meal a day, but he will still carry his lucky precious opals around with him in a matchbox or cigarette-tin.

You may be invited to sit on the bed, or on a packing-case. Elementary comforts make up his home. A concession to refinement may be a vase of plastic flowers on the table.

This is a typical story told by an opal miner: when he first went to Lightning Ridge, John lived in a caravan. His claim was nearby. As he found opal he put up his sign, "Opals for Sale", and his caravan was open for business.

He cut stones on hand-operated cutting equipment, which like most other miners, he kept in the open. Cutting equipment at Lightning Ridge is not usually given the almost antiseptic care

**Plate 10:** (*right*) The manpowered windlass has been a familiar landmark on Lightning Ridge fields for over fifty years.

**Plate 11:** (*below*) The petrol-powered winch is a modern refinement. The miners descend their hole in a swinging seat. All holes are equipped with a ladder.

that it receives in the cities. The dust at Lightning Ridge acts more as a polishing agent than as an abrasive. One wild night the caravan blew away, so John built himself a small shanty.

There are many "Johns" at Lightning Ridge. They come, and they go. They are never in one place for very long. So the shelters they build or lease are just shelters from the sun, or the rain (which rarely falls), but however temporary or makeshift these are their homes.

Not many new holes are dug these days. A new race of prospectors and miners has arrived. They are young, resourceful, and eager for quick rewards—without too much backache. Some are applying open-cut methods, successfully. Others are taking over deserted claims which have not been worked for years. They knock down the sandstone pillars left by the original owners of

A miner at Lightning Ridge looks through opal dirt for "colour" after it has been through his "puddler".

the claim to support the roof of the "room", far below the earth's surface.

Because of the strength of the sandstone, ceilings rarely cave in. When they do, it is a lucky miner who escapes unharmed. But there have been very few fatal casualties, and opal mining is considered to be the most pleasant and safest type of mining.

"Noodling" on the heaps is a favourite pastime of Aboriginals and tourists. They scratch happily away in the sizzling sun on the dazzlingly white heaps. They pick up pieces of "potch and colour" which have been overlooked by the old-timers who sank the shafts.

If it was a good productive hole some very good pieces of opal may be found. The old timers, like the new-comers of today, were always looking for the "big one".

# PUDDLERS

"Puddlers" are Lightning Ridge inventions. They are designed to flog away opal dirt and sandstone from precious opal.

A puddler, in theory, consists of a wire basket which holds four rubber paddles. These paddles are rotated swiftly, and are powered by an old car engine. Opal dirt from old heaps is shovelled into the basket, the paddles are set in motion, and the dirt is broken up by the force which is created. The heavier stones which then remain in the basket are tipped out and sorted. If any precious opal remains however, there is every chance of it being cracked or crazed by the whipping of the paddles.

This method is known as dry puddling, and is used by visiting amateur prospectors, or by local miners in times of drought. Amateur opal seekers engineer quite refined puddling models, but the general principle remains the same.

**Plate 12:** A valuable collection of magnificent opals, full of fire and colour.

The hotel at Lightning Ridge holds some amusing cartoons which capture the fleeting hopes and disappointment of opal seekers. They all carry their wistful message.

Wet puddling is preferred by professional miners, but the scarcity of water often makes this impossible. For wet puddling truckloads of opal dirt must be taken to a source of water, and water is a rare commodity in this dry country. Wet puddling is a much gentler way of recovering stones than the dry method.

The tiny town of Lightning Ridge is not without its sports and diversions. Once a year a race meeting is held, and this is a merry occasion. Crowds of miners, workers, farmers and tourists drive into Lightning Ridge for the day, coming from as far away as Coonamble, Coonabarabran, Dubbo and Walgett. They bring the kids, and the wife—and of course the wife wears her opal brooch, and rings.

There is a refreshment hut at the racecourse, and a stall for the beer. Bookmakers set up their stands under the yellow, green, red, blue, and multi-coloured umbrellas clustered near the finishing post. Bets are taken on interstate races as well, and the entire population enjoys the holiday atmosphere.

The six-furlong race track is straight. A commentator mounts his stand and shouts "They're off!" Children specially enjoy the events, and run to the rail to see two, or perhaps four horses thunder down the track, followed by a thick cloud of fine red dust. The main event on the race programme is fittingly called the "Opal Bracelet".

The race meeting officially ends when the kegs are empty. Later there is a dance and supper, with hired musicians. The revelry continues until the morning.

**Plate 13:** A gay crowd at the Lightning Ridge Race Meeting.

**Plate 14:** The horses run on a dusty track paced by small boys running on the grassed verge.

# VISITING COOBER PEDY

THE ROAD from Port Augusta to Coober Pedy is long, corrugated, and monotonous. Dead cars lie at intervals along the way. Only the tough survive. It is treacherous after rain, and at times becomes completely impassable. Stranded travellers have had to have supplies dropped to them from the air.

There are hundreds of miles of mulga which looks more dead than alive, as is its habit in dry weather. There are hundreds of miles of sunburnt stony ground with wispy yellow grasses, grey saltbush, and harsh spinifex. Flat-topped hills cradle shimmering white salt lakes which look like gigantic snowdrifts. Then more stones, more saltbush, more stalky mulga, more red sandhills, more red dust, red bushes, red trees. A red country . . . .

And the corrugations never improve, not even for one soothing half-mile.

Coober Pedy is in the low hills of the Stuart Range, 125 miles north of Tarcoola, and ninety-six miles west of William Creek Railway Station on the northern railway. It is 400 miles north-west of Port Augusta. Kingoonya, a railhead for the trans-continental railway, is the last road stop before Coober Pedy, and that is 180 miles away. A mail truck runs once a week between these two microscopic communities.

"Two lake drainage systems are divided by the hills of the Stuart Range. The opal field lies at the foot of a low scarp which forms the north-eastern slope of the range, and extends for forty miles north-westerly, with a width of about six to eight miles. Most of the mining takes place close to the

Coober Pedy, sun-drenched centre of South Australia's opal production.

Plate 15: Coober Pedy.

Plate 16: The main road.

scarp." (Information by courtesy of Sth Australian Mines Dept). The whole mining area is situated within the boundaries of Mount Clarence, a giant cattle station. Today about 700 people live at Coober Pedy.

The name Coober Pedy comes from an Aboriginal dialect and means "white fella live in hole in the ground"—inspired doubtless by the many white people who live in dugouts.

Temperatures average 115 degrees Farenheit during January and February, and sometimes throughout March. In July cold winds sweep across the bare countryside for several weeks. South-westerly winds prevail in winter, northerlies in summer.

A rough road leads north to Alice Springs. It is a lonely road, which passes through large station properties. The worst stretch of this road appears to be between Kingoonya and Coober Pedy, and travelling is necessarily slow.

The township of Coober Pedy in South Australia may come as a shock to the traditionalist. Several shops and hotels sprawl along the Stuart Highway for about a mile, 400 miles from Port Augusta and about 470 miles from Alice Springs. The dirt road is whipped to a red-dust-frenzy whenever a car zips along at racetrack speed, as is usual. On calm days the brilliant deep blue sky of the inland contrasts with the strong red-brown colours of the treeless Coober Pedy hills—these small, flat-topped hills which many people call home.

The shops carry ample provision for campers. It is no longer necessary to take food when visiting Coober Pedy. But a full water-bottle is always useful.

The only access to Coober Pedy is by air and road. It is not in the best interest of your car to take it to Coober Pedy, it is preferable to join a coach safari. Coaches are built more stoutly than cars; they stand up to the damaging corrugations on the dirt road much better and they carry more petrol and water. There are long stretches between the few oases where petrol may be obtained and rotting derelict cars and burnt-out chassis bear witness to those who didn't make it.

Even coaches may break down on this long hard run, for flying gibbers can pierce a petrol tank or a fuel line. Replacement parts may have to be flown in from other States, with a delay of several days. But at Coober Pedy time is of no consequence. The outside world is somewhere, but it's a long way off, and who should care about it anyway?

It is as well to restrict visits to the months from April to September. The heat can be unbearable in the summer months, especially when travelling.

Houses at Coober Pedy are carved out of the hills. These homes are comfortable, cool, and limitless in potential space. It is no trouble at all to excavate out another room when you need it. Beautiful furnishings, mats, drapes, and every known modern home convenience have been installed in many dugouts. These include refrigerators, stoves, and sewing machines. But there is no plumbing and no bathroom. There are many small gardens of heat-loving plants which must be carefully tended. These dugout homes when available, sell for about $1200.

These luxurious homes are in sharp contrast to those at Lightning Ridge and Queensland fields, where an above-ground shack remains a shack, with minimum furnishings. At these latter areas

**Plates 17, 18, 19:** (*opposite*) Three views of Coober Pedy township.

"Noodling" on the heaps.

the philosophy seems to be "I might strike it rich tomorrow, and then I'll move to the coast, so why bother to make a comfortable home for just one more day?"

Coober Pedy offers wonderful souvenirs to tourists who call here on the coach run from Alice Springs to Port Augusta. Underground jewellery shops provide interest and glamour, with demonstrations on opal-cutting for good measure.

The settlement has a percentage of resident Aboriginals. The children attend school with the white children. When not in school they "noodle" with the adults on the heaps and look for opal.

Dust storms are a common feature in this part of the inland. They whip up quickly, and visibility drops to a few yards or less. They may blow for days. Then the sky is red, the air is red, the dust fills nostrils and throats, and even filters into suitcases. Coarse grit and fine dust alike are lifted

into the air, and spread in red clouds—sometimes as far as New Zealand. The most comfortable places of refuge during a dust storm are mine shafts or dugout homes.

Accommodation at Coober Pedy is obtainable at three motels. This includes bed and breakfast, but without private bathroom amenities. Each motel has a dining room which caters for casual visitors as well as guests. Beer, wine, and spirits may be purchased from some stores and motels. Other local folk have comfortable cabins for hire, these mainly cater for the coach tourists on a one-night stay.

Many visitors still prefer to live under canvas. They take their own tents, or hire them. However, tents are useless in a wind or in a dust storm which could last a day or a week. Dust storms and willy-willies are fairly frequent in Australia's red heart.

Most coaches which take tours to the opal

**Plate 20:** Going down! Watching a descent.

**Plate 21:** Going up! Watching a "willy-willy".

Many dugouts are excavated out of a single hill.

Entrance to an underground jewellery shop, Coober Pedy.

fields are modern vehicles with soft seating, very necessary for this type of outback travel on corrugated roads.

On camping trips the passengers are responsible for their own catering throughout the journey. Quite often the coach company provides or hires tents, barbeques and general camp equipment. Passengers are advised to take a lilo air mattress (and perhaps a camp stretcher), sleeping bag, plastic groundsheet, two billies and a frypan. Besides this they need their own sleeping gear and personal luggage, eating and cooking utensils. Food is packed in plastic containers and stored under the seats. Most coaches carry their own refrigerators for storing passengers' butter and meat. They also carry large water containers.

A coach express service departs Adelaide twice a week, arriving at Coober Pedy, the following day. Fare, at the time of writing: single $16.00; double $30.75.

Access by air is available by means of an 8-seater twin-engined Cessna 402 aircraft, which leaves Adelaide Airport for Coober Pedy three times a week.

A church at Coober Pedy has been excavated as a dugout in a low hill. The altar has been attractively inlaid with slabs of jasper and other natural stone from the surrounding district. The walls are rough stone, just as Nature laid it down.

The township has two churches, a police station, hospital, Mines Department office, school, drive-in theatre, garage, bakery, butcher's shop, and three general stores where food, fresh milk (flown in from Adelaide), petrol and tyres may be obtained.

The Post Office at Coober Pedy is located in the Miners' Store. This is the real hub of the town. Miners from outlying fields swoop into town in a cloud of dust in their cars and jeeps,

Plates 22, 23: Coober Pedy architecture. Top: The underground church. Bottom: The Miner's Store.

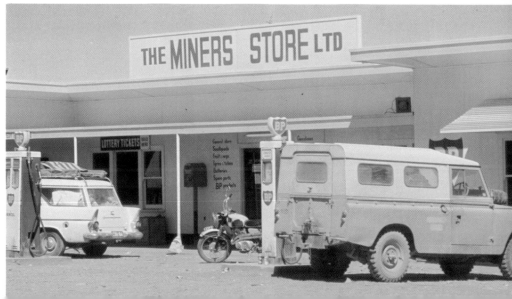

and stride into the store to collect their mail and provisions. If they have time to spare they may put a coin in the jukebox, or play a game of billiards. If they wish to sell their dugout or their car they can arrange for their "For sale" notice to be pinned to the door of the store.

The store has stocks of most things needed by a small community. Lamps, picks, rope, wire—everything for the miner. Food, drink, clothing, too. And cut opals.

Although the work of winning opal from a hostile countryside at Coober Pedy is carried on in all seriousness, the thousands of tourists who travel "through the centre" from April to September each year are welcomed.

So long as they keep well away from staked claims, especially at night, visitors to the fields are not worried. However, if they wander too near a claim which is producing good opal their souvenir might be a warning shot from a .303 rifle. Justice is swift and hard, even for the innocent.

Justice has been known to stalk the deliberate poacher in the form of a portion of a stick of gelignite dropped down the mine shaft after him. Who can say it was not an accident?

Tourists are advised to be courteous and circumspect, and ask *where* it is safe to noodle on the heaps. It is unwise to descend a hole unless with the express permission and in the presence of the owner.

Two supermarkets, a bakery and two general stores supply the necessities to local residents and tourists alike. They in turn are supplied by air and by the mail truck.

A visitor carries with him an impression of dust, flies, heat, and a sparse but friendly population. And, for the next 400 miles to Port Augusta, he dreams of a bath.

Travellers to the outback lose contact very quickly with their workaday world. They live in an atmosphere of fun, the unexpected, and of difficulty and resourcefulness. They become one

The hospital at Coober Pedy, The Flying Doctor calls here once a month.

Plate 25: "Noodling" among the mullock heaps in hopes of a lucky find.

A big heap of opal dirt, Coober Pedy.

with the strangeness of the inland. They learn to "rough it".

Some lapidary clubs in the Eastern States make a visit to Coober Pedy their main club event of the year. If their coach breaks down they all lend a hand. Who wants to go home, anyway? A club from NSW chartered a coach in August 1967. They made a twenty-seven hour dash to Port Augusta, where they stayed in a motel overnight. Theg completed the rest of the journey to Coober Pedy almost on schedule.

Bad luck caught up with them just six miles out of the town. It was six o'clock and a hot dinner was waiting for them at the hotel, but they didn't arrive at the hotel until nearly midnight. Fuel trouble had developed, and the starter motor burnt out. And of course there were no baths or showers after the long, hot, dustry trip. Just a small wash from a tap which was only just dripping.

The complete trip took nine days. The club members thoroughly enjoyed themselves. They were taken to parties by the miners, and invited into dugouts where wine was pressed upon them by hospitable New Australians. They found a *little* opal, purchased opals, and made many friends.

They scrambled up and down mullock heaps. They took a picnic lunch where white people have never picnicked before, and sat in the shelter of scrub mulga, amongst scorched pebbles in the shimmering heat of a winter's day. It was a trip to remember.

## CLAIMS AND MINERS' RIGHTS

AT ANDAMOOKA and Coober Pedy in South Australia a miner's right can be bought for 50 cents at the Department of Mines in Adelaide or Andamooka, or at the post office at Coober Pedy.

Only one claim can be held by one person at any one time, although up to four adjoining registered claims may be amalgamated with the permission of the Mining Warden. Claims can be held only in the names of persons holding current miners' rights. The Department requires at least one man for each claim to work constantly, e.g. for eight hours a day, on his claim, but this is not rigidly adhered to. Work must begin on a claim immediately it is pegged out.

40

**Plates 26, 27, 28:** Privileged visitors to Coober Pedy descend, by invitation, into the underground world of the opal miner.

An application for a precious-stones claim must be accompanied by the miner's right, together with the registration fee of $10. A sketch must accompany the application for registration of a mining claim, and show the north point, the position of the claim, with the measurements of the sides, and the distance and direction from other claims, numbered survey pegs, or wellknown landmarks.

Claims may be pegged out at any time, including Sundays. They must be square, with sides no longer than 150 feet. The number of the miner's right and the date of pegging must be clearly shown on each peg.

The penalty for illegal mining is a term of imprisonment for two years or a fine up to $600, as provided by the Mining Act. A penalty of $100 may be incurred for removing or damaging any boundary post or mark or peg on a current claim.

All visitors who intend fossicking for opal are required to purchase a miner's right.

A living site at Coober Pedy may be pegged for $6 a year by arrangement with the mining warden, or $20 per year for an acre.

One of the biggest lumps of opal ever found at Coober Pedy was the *Olympic Australis*. It was named in honour of the Olympic Games, held in Melbourne in the year it was discovered, 1956.

This is as it was told to us by the man who found it: "It was here in Coober Pedy, in August. Eleven o'clock at night, and freezing cold. We'd sunk a shaft twenty-eight foot six with pick and shovel—and we bottomed right on to opal. It was the first I'd ever found. I didn't know what it was when I first felt it with the pick—I was using candlelight.

"We were about to give up for the night. I was still down the shaft. Bert was the bucket man. 'Come on Frank!' he yelled down the hole. 'Aren't you coming up? It's getting late.'

" 'I just want to get this lump out,' I called back. 'I don't know what it is, but it's hard to move.'

"I tried to lever it out. 'Well, hit it with a pick,' Bert called down to me. He was tired and impatient. So I hit it with the pick. I was tired too, and gave it just one more try before I called it a day.

"I gave it a heavy tug, and the big lump came up with the pick. 'Send down something to haul this up in, Bert!' I called.

"Bert sent down the billy. 'Not that,' I shouted. 'Send down the four-gallon drum.'

"Bert forgot that he was cold. He forgot everything except that it looked as if we had something very interesting down that hole.

"We hauled up the lump. It was just like a loaf of bread."

Frank, his wife, and Bert were speechless for the next moment, as they held the candle close, and peered at the biggest opal in the world.

It was the largest opal that had been found to that date.

The mass of colour weighed 127 troy ounces.

But that was not all: underneath the big one, in a vertical trough, were six more opals. Two weighed 80 ounces each, one weighed 64 ounces, another weighed 60 ounces, and the smallest each weighed 45 ounces. A total of nearly 42 pounds of opal!

Frank and his wife used the opal—the big one—for a door-stop for a few weeks, then he decided to sell it.

The size of the *Olympic Australis* has since been eclipsed by opal found on other fields, but nevertheless, it is still a very famous piece of stone.

**Plates 29, 30, 31:** Bucket man at work, Coober Pedy. The mullock is hauled to the surface in a drum.

Diggings into a low hill, Coober Pedy.

A "name-stone" in the jargon of the opal fields, indicates a piece of opal which is big enough, or colourful enough to warrant the conferring of a name.

There is always a subdued atmosphere of expectancy on the opal fields, with an optimistic philosophy to temper disappointments and the blows of downright poverty when opal is elusive.

"This could be the day," is every miner's greeting to each new morn.

Naturally, each field has had at some time or other its itinerant rogues, camp followers, thieves and its cheats, but no more than any other place.

The opal mining partnership system usually works quite well. It has to. There must be trust, as one man chips away at the opal dirt 30 to 100 foot down a mine shaft, while the other is bucket-man at the top of the shaft; he empties out the loads of over-burden as it is hauled up on the winch from below.

Families live on the opal fields, and often the "missus" is as active as her husband in working their mine. Children go to school, but when school is out they are very adept and quick at finding opal on the mullock heaps. Girls often work the mine with their fathers, and groups of young women form partnerships amongst themselves.

The women who live and work on the opal fields earn the admiration of all who meet them. They do a man's work, live under conditions which would deter lesser souls, help with their children's schooling, drive hundreds of miles for supplies—and still remain cheerful.

There is a "feeling" that attaches itself to every

**Plates 32, 33, 34:** Holes and heaps at Coober Pedy.

opal field. It cannot be seen, or felt or heard. It is a subtle force that invisibly inhabits every hut and dugout, every shop, café and hotel, every automobile, every tourist coach.

It is the "presence of opal". And this is not as silly as it may sound.

The only excuse for the very existence of opal towns is, naturally enough, opal. For what other reason would folk inhabit a waterless, hot desert, where no crops will grow, except for the winning of this precious gem from the earth?

The dawn of each day brings fresh hope of finding "the big one". People greet each other with "Going to find the big one today?" where other folk say "Good morning".

They work, and work, and work. In temperatures that would deter city men and women they go into the wilderness, and climb down into the coolness of their shafts. In cramped quarters they chip gently away with infinite patience, hoping their exploring picks will touch on precious opal.

Talk is always of opal: where opal has been found, where opal should be found. Every opal miner suffers from supreme optimism: he *knows* he will find opal—it may take a little time, but he's prepared to wait.

At Lightning Ridge the hotel bar is the recognised opal miners' meeting place. At Coober Pedy and Andamooka supplies of wine and beer are stored in the coolness of the miner's dugout home, the better to support discussions about—opal.

Australia is the driest continent in the world, and in the inland water is almost non-existent. Water for isolated populations is sometimes brought from over a hundred miles away.

Bulldozing an "open cut" to opal level at Coober Pedy.

Plate 36: Miners checking on the bulldozer cut to see if the opal level has been reached.

Plate 35: A worked-out open cut, showing the geological strata.

WATER PRICES & SALE TIMES
MON. to FRI. 2·00 PM to 5·00 PM
SATURDAY 10·00 AM to 12·00 NOON
100 GALLONS 75 CENTS
44 GALL. DRUM 30 CENTS
20 GALLS. OR LESS 15 CENTS

At Coober Pedy, at the time of writing, water is rationed at the rate of 25 gallons per person per week. Quantities above this ration are sold at the following rates and times:

| Monday to Friday | 2 pm—5 pm |
| Saturday | 10 am—Noon |
| 100 gallons | 75 cents |
| 44 gallons | 30 cents |
| 20 gallons | or less, 15 cents |

The town water supply holds about 500,000 gallons. One inch of rain in a drizzle will fill it, or a 30 point cloudburst. This is augmented by one of the largest solar stills in the world, with an approximate capacity of 50,000 gallons per day.

Coober Pedy opal fields abound in gypsum and jasper. Precious opal is known to form on both materials.

Jasper, also formed by deposition of silica from solutions, is very different from opal. It is cryptocrystalline and belongs to a definite crystal system. Opal has no crystal system. Jasper has a hardness of 7, opal has a hardness of $5\frac{1}{2}$ to $6\frac{1}{2}$ on Mohs' scale. Jasper is solid, opaque, and has no play of colour like opal. It has a dull colour-range of cream to brown, cream to red, green and blue. The jasper deposits are sometimes more than 100 feet thick, above opal level.

**Plates 37, 38, 39:** Coober Pedy water reservoir and solar still.

Mud shells encased in sandstone.

Aboriginal artifacts fashioned from jasper in eras long past abound in the surrounding country. They include spearheads, knives, axeheads and circumcision stones.

Countless thousands of shells have been completely replaced by precious opal. One field alone alone has been named the "Shell Patch" because most of the opal found there is in the form of fossil fresh-water and sea-shells.

About twenty miles from Coober Pedy a gigantic bank of sediments, left by receding tides in a bygone geological period, curves as the waves shaped it, like the beach sands of today. Incredible numbers of "mud" shells lie here, together with many other types of fossils.

Kaolin, a silicate of aluminium, is white to pink in colour, and is known on the field as opal dirt. Opal has formed in its cracks and fissures.

Plates 40, 41, 42: Material associated with opal. *Left:* fibrous gypsum. *Below:* Kaolin. *Right:* Jasper (worked pieces used as weapon heads by the aboriginal tribes).

# THE "BREAKAWAY"

OPAL is known to exist over a large area in South Australia, but lack of water is a serious deterrent to prospecting.

Twenty miles west of Coober Pedy a remarkable land formation known locally as "The Breakaway" provides enthralling views of an eroded land. Prospectors and miners weep because it has been eroded below the possible opal level. Doubtless, millions of dollars' worth of opal once formed here, but wind and water through the ages took their inexorable toll.

For geologists and photographers "The Breakaway" is a dream valley. It is surrounded by low, flat hills. Sunburnt black stones cover the ground between thin stunted mulga.

In the valley itself, erosion-resistant mounds of white and yellow rock stand sentinel to a bygone age. This place is one of Nature's masterpieces but it lies hidden and remote in the innermost recesses of the Australian continent.

Breakaway landscape.

**Plate 43:** Colourful, eroded landscape of "The Breakaway".

Treeless landscape at Coober Pedy.

# FLOWERS OF THE INLAND

COOBER PEDY itself has two small trees. One grows over the doorway of the underground church. The other is farther away from the town.

The ground is stony and brown, but here and there flowers of the Australian desert bloom in shades of yellow, blue, white and red. They are hardy little beauties.

After a shower of rain the ten-day grass springs up. If it does not receive another shower within ten days (often a forlorn hope) it withers and dies.

Several miles out from the town short green eucalypts, mulga and tufty yellow grasses soften the landscape, as they follow the watercourses.

In central-western Queensland, near the opal fields, flowers have been scarce during the last nine years of drought. But after good and consistent rains in 1968 the country sprang into bloom again and was covered by miles and miles of wildflowers.

54

**Plate 44:** Yellow Desert Cassia.

**Plate 45:** Scarlet Sturt's Desert Pea.

# VISITING ANDAMOOKA

OPAL AT ANDAMOOKA was not discovered until 1930. The fields lie on a comparatively flat table-land, west of Lake Torrens, about ninety-eight miles by road north-east of Pimba railway station on the Transcontinental railway. A graded road leads from Port Augusta to the Woomera/Arcoona Station turn-off, but from Arcoona Station to the opal fields the road is classed as a "pastoral track".

In normal weather the track affords reasonably comfortable access, but in dry weather it can be very sandy and dusty. In all weathers it is very stony.

At Andamooka a number of dugouts are available to visitors, who may hire them from about $12.00 per week. These are similar to those dugouts used by the opal miners. Many visitors camp out. As on other opal fields, there appear to be thousands of holes, on several different fields, and several miles apart.

The opal diggings and "township" are scattered, and cover a large area. There is a post office, provision store, general store, chemist, service station, Red Cross centre, police station, drive-in theatre, cool drink factory, and a butcher. About two hundred people live permanently on the field.

There is a school. Dances are held occasionally, also film shows. Some very fine homes have been built at Andamooka, some with air conditioning, electric light—and private aeroplane parked outside.

In addition to the 8-seater aircraft which serves Coober Pedy and calls at Andamooka, a 5-passenger Cessna 206 operates a twice weekly round trip service between Adelaide and Anda-mooka. Fare, at the time of writing: Single $28.00; Return $56.00. Weekend opal tours are conducted by the South Australian Tourist Bureau. Fare, at the time of writing: $50.00 for an adult. On some public holidays, week-end camping tours to Andamooka are organised by the Bureau.

Andamooka has a good supply of River Murray water, which is obtained from Woomera by the Andamooka Progress Association. A small charge is made for its supply.

The intense heat of the inland has forced most people on the South Australian opal fields to make their homes underground. Low hills have been tunnelled and excavated to provide cool shelter from temperatures of up to 140 degrees. These dugouts have rooms like those of any conventional house. Some are excavated with only a roof constructed above ground.

Kitchen, diningroom, lounge and bedrooms are dug out; bathrooms are usually missing, for what use is a bathroom when there is so very little water? The motels have good bathrooms, but the taps dribble only a few drops of water to remind the guest to be prudent in its use.

Medical doctors have tried opal mining, and have also practised on the opal fields, but medical attention is usually provided by the Flying Doctor service. The doctor visits the four-bed Coober Pedy hospital once a month. The people in the inland fear appendicitis above most other ill-nesses.

Aboriginals "noodle" for opal on the heaps, and often make good finds. They may sell their opal for cash, or exchange it for booze. When they receive cash every last member of the tribe hears about it, and descends to share in the bonanza. It is not unusual for large sums of money to be

**Plate 46:** Milk opal (left).

**Plate 47:** Matrix opal (below).

spent on drink and frivolities. The Government has provided homes, but few Aboriginals use them. Many prefer to sleep in old cars or in the open.

Andamooka opal is prized for its clear bright colours. It is eminently suitable for douplet-making, as well as for superb solids.

Miners usually work in partnership on the opal fields. Choosing a partner is a serious business. The two men must trust each other—implicitly. The choice of a bad partner can be disastrous. For example, one miner may show *all* his opal, but a bad partner may show only a token amount and pocket the rest.

When a good piece is found, the two partners sometimes take it along to the cutter together. When the opal is sold they split the proceeds.

They may blow the lot as soon as possible. They may give a party, and hire a chef from the city for a week, or they may "shout" the locals and paint the town red. When the money has gone, they toss off their hangover and look for more opal.

Not all miners are improvident but they are all strong believers in luck. They *feel* luck. They know "when they are on a winning streak, and cannot go wrong". They "know" when every hole they touch will produce opal. They "feel" when their luck on a field has run out, and they drift off to another field for a "spell".

One miner had a lucky strike, so he left Lightning Ridge and moved to Queensland for a few years. He knew his hole had more opal in it, but he wanted to live it up in the cities for a little

Entrance to a dugout, Andamooka. A "show" opal mine. (Photograph by courtesy of South Australian Tourist Bureau.)

**Plate 48:** Opals from South Australian fields.

while. Soon enough he was broke again, and returned to the Ridge to work his hole. A shop had been built over it!

In the old days, the town of Lightning Ridge was situated at the "Three Mile". The old hotel was demolished long ago, but cut stones are still being discovered on the site—dropped from the pockets of miners of long ago.

For hundreds of acres at the Three Mile, Four Mile, Nine Mile, Bald Hill, Pony Fence, and Telegraph Line, nearly every blade of grass has been covered with white opal dirt. Windblown seeds may germinate near derelict holes, and then stunted grasses and trees struggle for a foothold on life.

# THE BUYING AND SELLING OF OPAL

ONE MUST BE A LITTLE CAREFUL when buying rough opal.

Look out for "ginger whisker"—this is the name some miners give to crazed but colourful matrix. It is worthless for cutting good stones, yet may be offered at high prices.

Rough opal for sale is sometimes hard to find, especially if interstate or overseas buyers have recently been on the field. But the visitor to Coober Pedy or other working opal fields with a few days to spare will sooner or later meet up with a miner with rough opal for sale. The price may

A miner's dwelling at the Andamooka Opal Field, South Australia. (Photograph by courtesy of the South Australian Tourist Bureau.)

**Plate 49:** A "parcel" of good average quality rough opal from the Andamooka field.

be a definite figure, or be subject to bargaining, so do not be surprised if you cannot get a simple answer to your question of "How much?"

"I'll have to see my partner," is a good hedge by the seller. A would-be buyer can be driven to exasperation by this "I'll see my partner" business. Especially if the partner wants to "jack up" the price.

You can buy a small parcel, or a large parcel, but rarely a broken parcel. If you *are* allowed to buy one or two selected pieces, be prepared to pay a *lot* more for them.

Itinerant and unscrupulous drifters find their way to the opal fields. They pose as *bona fide* buyers and sellers. They are often hard to recognise, because they seem to be such genuine and friendly fellows.

Once, a fine sincere chap in the opal business offered to sell a parcel of cut stones for a friend, and that was the last ever seen of the opals or the fine sincere chap. When enquiries were made, it was found that he had played the same game with many other opal dealers in Australia, and owed them thousands of dollars. He had taken opals from them to sell on commission, but always failed to settle any of the accounts.

✤✤✤✤✤✤✤✤✤✤✤✤

The NSW Department of Mines gives the following information:

The common method of mining is to sink a small shaft through the overlying sandstone to the level of the "opal dirt". This is tested at the base of the shaft, and if no opal is found the shaft is then abandoned and another hole dug nearby.

Once the opal dirt is struck at the bottom of a shaft great care has to be taken that worthwhile gems are not broken by contact with a pick or shovel. The opal dirt is literally shaved with a pick until opal is encountered.

A mining claim.

**Plate 50:** A piece of opal larger than man's fist—value about $1500.

# VISITING THE QUEENSLAND OPAL FIELDS

THERE CAN BE no more rewarding journey for Australian or overseas tourists to make than to the opal fields of NSW, South Australia or Queensland, but in Queensland especially is seen the real outback, with its ultimate isolation and serenity.

The visitor will experience the overwhelming hospitality of the opal miners and feel the genuine friendship of the people who live and work in these lonely outposts.

During days that are long and tranquil and untroubled one is privileged to share in the excitement of fossicking, and perhaps in the thrill of finding some opal. There is always someone

Portion of the small settlement of Kynuna in the Queensland opal belt. Although close to the Diamantina River, which spreads to more than eighty miles wide when in flood, Kynuna lies in one of the driest parts of the interior of Queensland.

with opal for the visitor to look at, or perhaps buy. Visits to the opal fields are recalled long after lesser experiences have faded.

Tourists may look for opal all through central-western Queensland, from Yowah to Winton, but they are advised to take the following precautions, reproduced here by courtesy of the *Queensland Mining Journal:*

As conditions in any area can change overnight with changing weather conditions, all people planning visits to opal or other gem and mineral fields are advised to contact the local police authorities before venturing into remote and unfamiliar terrain. A few words of advice obtained in this manner can be the means of preventing exposure to the multitude of dangers which await the inexperienced traveller in the outback.

Travelling west from Charleville, the 153 miles from Quilpie to Windorah are almost completely surfaced with bitumen and this road can be used to best advantage. A reasonable dry weather road extends from Windorah to Longreach through Jundah, a distance of 192 miles—consequently it is possible to get by car to Longreach under favourable weather conditions.

However, Beef Roads represent only a proportion of the routes leading to and through out back areas; consequently any extensive itinerary designed to explore remote regions of far western Queensland, even where Beef Roads have been constructed, will involve travelling many miles of bush roads, which could present problems to motorists inexperienced in back country driving.

Conditions are not yet suitable for city motorists to travel extensively through the

**Plate 51, 52:** Rough opal showing good colours.

**Plate 53:** (*overleaf*) Opal in ironstone matrix from Duck Creek field, Queensland.

outback, but if a trip must be undertaken, it is wise to be prepared for emergencies. The following points are worth noting:

*The Vehicle:* The car must be in top class. Outback motoring can be tough, so it is imperative that the vehicle be sound mechanically and have good tyres, including two spares. Although cars with small wheels can tackle most road conditions they are not recommended for outback travel—they bog too easily in sand or mud and do not stand up well to the strains imposed by rocks and corrugations.

*Take precautions:* The first thing any motorist venturing into remote areas must keep in mind is that distances between towns, settlements, or roadside stops at which water and petrol can be got are often great. A few spare cans of water and petrol and a reserve food supply could easily mean the difference between an uncomfortable and expensive delay—or even serious trouble—and a safely completed journey.

*Bogging in Sand, Mud:* If bogged, first try deflating the tyres to about half normal pressure. This increases the effective gripping surface. If this fails, raise the vehicle with the jack and lodge hard material under the wheels to give the tyres something on which to grip. Suitable hard materials usually found in the outback include grass, leaves, sticks, stones, small logs—even ant-beds.

*Mechanical Breakdowns* Precaution is the best safeguard against mechanical breakdown. Before setting out, have the vehicle thoroughly checked and any necessary repairs effected. As far as possible, get to know how to attend to minor repairs on your own.

As an added safeguard, carry a selection of spare parts: patches and a spare tube, coil, two spark plugs, condenser, fan belt, radiator hoses, a set of distributor points, headlight bulbs and fuses.

Other items likely to be very useful in remote areas and which should always be carried are:

Extra tyre and tube (additional to the normal spare).

Extra jack with a suitable base plate, to stop it sinking into sand or mud.

Gallon tin of engine oil.

Axe to cut bushes and timber.

Shovel to clear away mud or sand if the vehicle is bogged.

Good kit of tools, including a tyre pump.

Length of $\frac{3}{4}''$ plastic tubing.

*Breakdowns in remote areas:* Sometimes a vehicle will sustain damage which puts it out of service many miles from help. If this happens:

Stay with the vehicle while awaiting help.

Conserve water and food supplies.

Don't attempt to walk about in the heat, or in any other way exert the body so that it will need more water, which already may be in short supply.

Before setting out into remote areas, tell some reliable person where you intend to go, the route to be taken, when you expect to get there, and when you expect to return. Then if your arrival or return should be overdue, a search-party would know where to start looking without delay.

Above all, if you do become lost or stranded, stay with your vehicle and don't attempt to walk out. A motor vehicle is much easier to find than a human being walking.

Conserve your water supply. If it threatens to run out, remember an extra supply can be obtained by draining the radiator.

# YOWAH OPAL FIELDS

THE YOWAH OPAL FIELDS are usually easy to reach, except in times of rain. The most direct route from Sydney is through Bourke, Cunnamulla, and Eulo.

The road to Eulo by way of Bourke is mainly sealed, but there are breaks of sixty miles or more of dirt road. This is quite passable in dry weather, but after or during rain it is always wise to make enquiries about the state of the road from the police, Dept of Main Roads (Bourke), or local service-station personnel.

From Eulo to Yowah the road and surrounding soil are vermilion red. The terrain is varied, with undulating hills, eucalypts of medium height, and grey acacias. In times of drought the country is cracked, parched and stark. After rain it is beautiful, with every turn in the road presenting a Nature-canvas of graded bright greens, greys, and yellows and reds. Miles of wildflower carpets will appear after several good showers, and thousands of varieties of succulents cover the ground with varying leaf colours, the flowers being white, yellow, and lilac.

The Yowah fields are fifty-four miles from Eulo. The opal found here is mainly the "kernels" of Yowah "nuts". Opal is also found in matrix and in "pipes". The "nuts" are unique to this area. The tortuous dirt road leads through large sheep properties. The opal fields themselves are situated on a sheep station.

People visiting the field from Eulo first take the road to Thargomindah. (Eulo is forty-nine miles from Cunnamulla on the Thargomindah road.) Then turn *right* eleven miles out, on to the Quilpie-Toompine Road. Twenty-six miles along this road turn *left* off the Quilpie-Toompine road. Three miles along there is a further left turn to the opel field. Another left turn in another four miles. Three miles further on, turn left at the "miners' mailbox". Seven miles along the road the first of the miners' shacks and tents appear. This is Yowah. (Several gates must be opened, and *closed*, after passing through.)

This field is particularly popular with people from Victoria. Besides the call of opal, they enjoy the warmth of the central Queensland climate.

Housing on the field does not follow any planned and standardised pattern. The miners, both men and women, live in makeshift shelters. They, in common with miners on other fields, consider their days on the opal fields to be a temporary phase of life. Huts, tents, caravans, old buses, or a

A happy youngster living on the opal fields.

Plate 54: A split-open "Yowah nut".

Plate 55: Boulder opal, showing veinlets of precious opal in ironstone matrix.

combination of all these may be called "home". Only about fifteen miners work this field permanently, but campers and visitors swell the population numbers to about 100.

Water is no problem at Yowah. The bore, which produces 18,000 gallons each hour, was put down about 1911, and runs continually with sweet, clear, albeit hot water. It is good for drinking, washing, and bathing, and the Yowah people consider themselves fortunate.

Children who live at Yowah with their parents do their school lessons by correspondence. And they can study Nature on the spot, for the wild green parakeets, pink galahs, emus, kangaroos, lizards, even snakes, are ever close at hand.

Children hunt for opal too. Some excellent pieces were once found by nine-year-old twins, Alana and Peter. These lay only eight inches below the surface. Another little boy, all of four years old climbs hand over hand down a rope thirty feet to the bottom of his mother's shaft.

# THE YOWAH
# "KERNEL BAND"

(By courtesy of the *Queensland Mining Journal*)
THE YOWAH OPAL FIELD is in the Cunnamulla Mining District of the Desert Sandstone series. Here the precious opal found is mostly formed as centres or kernels of small nodules of siliceous ironstone. Some of the richest deposits ever found in Queensland were on this field. The "Kernel band" occurs usually between twenty-five and forty feet in depth and consists of a bed of concretionary nodules closely packed in soft clayey sandstone. The beds dip in different parts of the field.

Detached scattered nodules of siliceous iron-

stone are seen above the main band as high as eight feet and in some cases a second band or nest of nodules is seen about two feet above the main one. Examples of opal being found as the kernel of concretionary nodules occur in several of the opal fields, but the occurrence of the nodules in such numbers in the form of a definite bed or stratum is altogether unique to Yowah.

The compacted mass forming this bed of kernel boulders varies from six inches up to two feet in thickness, and has a conglomerate-like appearance. The matrix is made up of a somewhat friable sandy mass containing a large proportion of clay in irregular masses and rounded lumps. The kernel boulders are undoubtedly of concretionary origin formed *in situ*. They vary from about a quarter of an inch up to six or eight inches in diameter, and have a spherical or ellipsoidal shape. The chocolate or brown colour is due to the presence of oxide of iron.

These kernels have evidently been deposited from the outside towards the centre, and have alternate rings of dark and light-brown colour, which varies in composition from a siliceous ironstone to a ferruginous opal. In the centre is generally a kernel of pure opal. Occasionally there is a layer of opal between the outer skins or at the outer edge, and veinlets of opal often ramify through the matrix.

The centre of these boulders is not always filled in the same manner, and examples occur of the kernel being composed as follows:
  a) of precious opal;
  b) of common opal, smoky, clear, or glassy, yellowish, or resin opal, white, yellow, and black;
  c) of the same material as the outer portion, sometimes shot through with veinlets of precious opal;

**Plates 56, 57:** "Yowah nuts", showing kernels of precious opal.

d) of opal, generally of the glassy variety, but having the kernel quite loose in the shell;

e) of a fine white powder;

f) of a small quantity of fluid like water;

g) or the boulders may be quite hollow and have no kernel.

## EULO OPAL FESTIVAL

EULO was once a staging post for the Cobb & Co coaches bound for Hungerford and Thargomindah. The tiny town is rich in history.

The annual rainfall is twelve inches, except in times of drought, when it is considerably less. All the water used by the townsfolk comes from artesian bores. It is sweet, cool, and soft. Eulo is a town of blue skies, wide open spaces, and complete freedom.

The first Opal Festival of Cunnamulla and Eulo, in Queensland, was held between these two country towns, nearly fifty miles apart, on 16, 17 and 18 August, 1968. Hundreds of people travelled to Eulo, danced until 3 am, then drove the fifty miles home again, as is the wont of people who live in the outback.

This was the Festival Programme:

Friday 16: Dance at Eulo Hall, and crowning of Opal Queen.

Saturday 17: Paroo Polocross Championships at Cunnamulla. Procession through streets of Cunnamulla, with decorated floats, Mardi Gras. Fancy-dress ball.

Sunday 18: Boomerang throwing and Aboriginal singing. Visit to Yowah fields to fossick, and inspect miners' opal. Barbeque lunch. Demonstration of opal cutting by miners. Tea and Campfire Singing at Yowah.

At the Festival dance the Minister for Tourism in Queensland crowned the Opal Queen. He then announced the Opal Festival of Eulo and Cunnamulla to be officially open.

**Plate 58:** The Eulo Queen Hotel.

**Plate 59:** Eulo general store.

The town of Eulo consists of a hotel, café, post office, police station, store and community hall. 1968 was Eulo's centenary year.

The Eulo Opal Queen crowning and the festival is based on this colourful local story:

The "challenge of the inland" in the early days of Australia's history produced many men and women whose lives have become legends. Now they live on in the minds of the people who knew them, and who have talked of their deeds to their children.

Such a person was the Eulo Queen. She was a glamorous personality and the most talked-of woman in central-western Queensland in the 1880s. She was the only white woman in this remote area during this time and drovers, opal gougers, goldminers and shearers have all contributed to the romantic story of the "Eulo Queen."

Very few facts can be verified about her life. Isobel MacIntosh was her name and she was a striking beauty with blonde hair and grey eyes. She was witty and vivacious, and she was a fine horsewoman. As an immigrant girl she secured her first position in Australia as governess on Bungiwagga Station, out from Bourke. Here she met and married the station overseer.

The couple moved to Cunnamulla in Queensland, and managed the Cobb & Co store. Here they saved sufficient money to buy a hotel at Eulo, fifty miles away.

The surrounding country was divided into large cattle stations, and three opal fields were discovered about forty miles from Eulo. These fields then supported nearly 300 miners. With a bi-weekly coach service coming into the town, the MacIntosh's hotel prospered. Isobel became the toast of the drovers and the miners. She acquired the finest collection of opals in Australia, and she wore her opal jewellery as she served in the bar of the hotel. It is claimed that men travelled hundreds of miles to see her. She was soon the "Eulo Queen".

Isobel became wealthy. She bought another hotel, and ran a store in Eulo, She speculated in

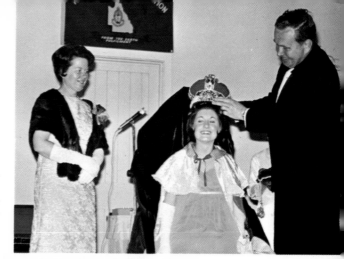

Plate 60: (*right*) The crowning of the Opal Queen at Eulo.

Plate 61: (*below*) This is a rich and intricately decorated trinket box, believed to have once belonged to the "Eulo Queen". Provision has been made in the velvet lining for a tiara to rest on. The box is made of ebony, inlaid with ivory and boulder opal from Queensland. It was recently rediscovered by a lover of antiques and opal.

Mud shells.

minerals, and although she was not always lucky she was a shrewd businesswoman. Tales of her generosity tell of her kindness to starving miners. She could judge the character of an out-of-luck opal gouger and would stake him until his luck improved. Records show that she had three husbands over the years she spent at Eulo.

Towards the end of her life her own luck changed. Fires ravaged her hotels—she was forced to sell her opal jewellery and the final act in Isobel's drama was tragic. She died in complete poverty in a home for the aged in Brisbane.

A rebuilt portion of the original Eulo Hotel still stands.

# SHELLS

SHELLS are numerous in the dry Australian inland, for huge seas once swept over the continent. As the ages passed millions of sea creatures were isolated and marooned when the seas began to recede. Eventually they dried completely and the inland is now a dry desert country.

In time the ground waters, holding silica in solution also evaporated. They left behind the phenomenon known as "opal". Hydrated silica was deposited in fissures in sandstone, on gypsum, and on jasper. It entered the shells of the stranded marine creatures. Sometimes it replaced the entire shell, sometimes only the thin hard outer covering. (These latter are called "skin shells" by miners on the field.)

Not all shells were completely or even partly opalised. Millions were fossilised by the pressure of mud only, and although they retain their shell shape and characteristic markings, they are known as "mud shells", and are of value only to the collectors of inland fossil souvenirs.

In February 1965 a London newspaper reporting a gem sale read: "A black four-inch-long opal which formed part of the opalised rib of a Plesiosaurus, a prehistoric animal dug up in Australia in 1928, sold for £6,200."

# THE NATURE AND ORIGIN OF OPAL

By P. J. Darragh and A. J. Gaskin

MOST OPAL is composed of packed arrays of myriads of tiny spheres of hydrous silica, less than 0.0005 millimetres (5000 Å) in diameter. In some varieties of common opal the spheres are less than 0.0001 mm (1000 Å) in diameter and are hence too small to produce a play of colours by the diffraction of visible wavelengths of light, regardless of whether the spheres are stacked in regular arrays or not. In potch, the constituent spheres are generally of a suitable diameter (2000–4000 Å) but irregularities in shape and size, or the presence of fine impurities such as clay minerals, prevent the attainment of the regular packing structure that is necessary for diffraction (Fig. 1).

Varieties such as wood opal and opalised bone can have their internal stacking sequences disrupted by the remnants of cell walls, although in some such pseudomorphs the leaching of the original substance has been complete enough to leave clear spaces sufficiently large for the introduction and precise arrangement of spheres of the right size to give good diffraction effects (Fig. 2).

Large pieces of precious opal are typically formed in clear cavities in rocks, where the growth of spheres has proceeded without interruption and there has been room for processes of sizing and stacking to go on in an optimum manner.

Electron micrograph shows the irregularly shaped and arranged spheres in potch.

Scale: 1 inch = 1 micron. (Fig. 1.)

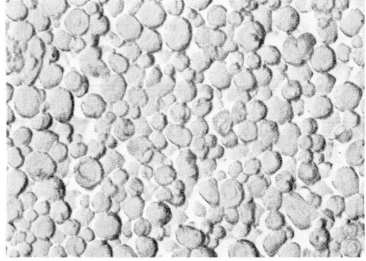

78

**Plate 63:** Opals from the South Australian fields.

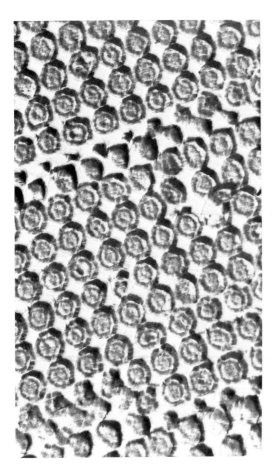

This electron micrograph shows the regular shape of spheres and the high degree of order in packing in a precious opal section of fossil bone. The shell structure of the spheres is clearly visible. Scale: 1 inch = 1 micron. (Fig. 2.)

Although it was evident from quite an early stage in the work that the spheres in opal were large colloidal sol particles and that "fire" in opal depended not only on the size, but on the perfection of shape and arrangement of these particles, it was far from clear why they grew in such a regular manner. After some initial speculations on this problem, including thoughts of a possible organic origin, two lines of investigation were pursued, first by attempts to grow such particles in the laboratory and second, by studying as many different specimens of opal as possible, both in collections and in typical field occurrences. We would like to take this opportunity to thank firms and members in the Association for their generosity in loaning many of the specimens that were examined in these studies.

Laboratory work showed that it was not difficult to take an aqueous silica sol containing, initially, very small particles, having diameters less than 100 Å, and by long-continued heating and concurrent introduction of fresh colloidal silica, gradually to increase the size of the particles as the overall silica content of the system was raised by progressive evaporation of water. The mechanism of particle growth may be compared with the polymerisation of organic molecules.

The course of growth of the sol particles was followed in all these experiments by electron microscopy and this showed that particles grew smoothly and relatively rapidly to diameters of 100–400 Å but then tended to aggregate into clusters rather than grow larger as individuals. Since the small "primary" particles are spherical, the "secondary" aggregates are spherical clusters made up of a few core particles surrounded by successive shells of primary spheres, like the

**Plate 64:** Rough opal from Coober Pedy.

structure of an onion. The sizes of the secondary aggregates are then determined largely by the number of shells.

During a year of successive trials and with many modifications of techniques, the art of producing spherical silica aggregates was mastered sufficiently to permit the preparation of suspensions of regularly shaped and sized spheres (Fig. 3).

When these were carefully sedimented by long standing, layers showing opaline "fire" were formed where the particles settled into regularly-arranged beds having the correct order of spacing to generate optical diffraction effects. Subsequently, the problem of removing the water from these soft beds was overcome and means found for cementing the arrays of particles together to produce a solid mass still showing "fire". The physical properties of our product are of course somewhat different from those of natural opal. It is not as hard and strong and it is not in such a stable form as the natural stone, hence would not at present seem to be an attractive proposition for use as a synthetic gem. Although it appears unlikely that important amounts of synthetic opal could be made without a great deal of further developmental effort, the CSIRO has applied for patent protection, with the object of being perhaps in a position to exercise some control over production should the need ever arise.

As the work concerned with the basic chemistry of production of opaline silica progressed, the field evidence relating to the origin of the natural stone was re-examined in the light of the main factors thought to be of potential significance. Some of the results of both lines of investigation have been published in a scientific article. Opal occurrences are known to be typically at shallow depths below an arid ground surface, though some levels are worked as far down as 80 feet and, rarely, to 120 feet. The cover rocks are, or have been, highly porous. In the main fields the opal levels are just above beds of bentomitic clay of low permeability, which act both as local traps for ground water and also as a source of silica in aqueous solution. Opal occurs as a filling in cavities of all sizes and we are satisfied that it has been produced, in general, by the long-continued concentration of local siliceous ground-waters through evaporation of water through the porous cover rock. In principle, the natural process of formation is similar to that which we have developed in the laboratory for growing silica spheres in the preparation of synthetic opal.

If the natural deposition of opal depends essentially on the common phenomenon of evaporation of water from sub-surface silica solutions held in rock cavities, why is opal rare? The answer appears to involve a complex of more or less independent factors. First, because the solubility of silica in water is low (about 0.01%) a good deal of water has to evaporate to produce any quantity of the mineral. Since sufficient rock cover must exist to isolate a suitable host cavity from seasonal effects of flooding and desiccation which could destroy the special qualities of the stone, evaporation is greatly impeded. However, in special situations, where very porous cover rocks lie above limited but persistent supplies of siliceous ground-water in arid areas, conditions can favour the steady accumulation of significant amounts of silica sol particles in these concentrating solutions. Even so, the rate of deposition of such particles to form layers of opal would be slow, according to some calculations we have made for the main Australian fields, using data on the permeability and

**Plate 65:** "Solids" opals cut from good quality South Australian rough.

Spheres grown in the laboratory, show composite particles very rarely seen in precious opal. Scale: 1 inch = 1 micron. (Fig. 3.)

thickness of the cover rock, the aridity of the ground surface, and the temperature gradient expected to obtain down to the depths of the opal levels. Periods of the order of several million years could have been involved in the formation of appreciable amounts of the stone in isolated cavities at the deepest levels.

A further requirement for the deposition of precious opal is that the silica spheres grown in ground-waters must be settled out of suspension on reaching a critical size and allowed to pack into regular geometrical arrays with minimum disturbance by earth movements, clay particles, salt crystals, or any other contaminants or interfering factors. Ordinary forms of opaline silica are very common in arid regions and are composed of spheres analogous to those in precious opal, but because the spheres are distorted in shape, or too small, or have their packing disrupted from a regular pattern by foreign particles, these varieties are not comparable with precious opal in regard to the diffraction of visible light. Even under conditions favourable to the deposition of precious opal, there is ample evidence in the main fields that host cavities have occasionally been flooded or dried out, resulting in layered discontinuities in the texture of the stone or the presence of shrinkage cracks filled with later opal.

Examination of textural features in opal from collections and as it occurs in the working face in diggings, has given the impression that the colloidal suspensions from which it formed were not free-moving liquids but had the consistency of thin jellies. Some of the flow effects, preserved in the stone by subsequent hardening processes, give distinctive and often attractive characteristics to large specimens but in general the results of movements that occurred whilst the opal was

**Plate 66:** Pieces of "skin shell" from Coober Pedy opal fields.

in the early soft state have been deleterious. The consistency of the gel and its freedom from impurities or strong flow movements have been, in our opinion, important basic influences on the characteristics of the opal in its ultimate form. Silica spheres growing in very thin media have, for example, settled out as a layer across the floor of a host cavity before attaining the correct size ranges necessary for the production of regular arrays capable of diffracting visible light. On the other hand, spheres growing in relatively stiff gels have commonly been prevented from settling and gradually sorting out into precise arrays on a size basis. Through undisturbed progressive sedimentation of spheres in gel media of the correct consistency we can, however, visualise conditions suitable for the concurrent growth and downward migration of particles of a uniform size within a single host cavity. From examinations of the basic structure of many specimens showing little or no fire, we have found that lack of precise sizing and regular arrangement of spheres is a common reason for the failure of potch to show the special optical features of precious opal. Note, however, that the special requirements imposed on gel consistency in the natural system do not apply to the preparation of synthetic opal, where the spheres can be grown to correct size in a stirred free-flowing liquid medium in one vessel, then transferred to a still vessel for settling into regular layers over a period of some weeks, using a solution as thin as water.

The concept of spheres growing by aggregation of primary colloidal particles, then sinking through a thin gel to build up layers of sized and regularly arranged diffracting objects was reached partly by examination of synthetic systems and partly through the field evidence. Natural features seen in precious opal could be understood in terms of this hypothesis or duplicated in the laboratory. For example, opal in the field commonly shows a horizontally layered structure with characteristics originating in the process of sedimentation of the component spheres. The largest spheres, which can diffract red light, are generally at the base of specimens which show a vertical graduation in quality and colour of fire. Smaller spheres, which had slower settling rates and hence tended to concentrate towards the tops of specimens, can only diffract green and violet light so the colour of the fire typically changes from red, at the base of a layer, to green-violet at the top. Where green-diffracting spheres settled at an early stage through a rather thin gel, the upper parts of the resulting specimens have been observed to show only violet fire, or in some cases no visible fire at all if the sizes of spheres in the upper part of the specimens pass below the diffraction limits for the shortest wavelengths of visible light. This simple phenomenon of differential settling is of course over-ridden quite easily by other factors such as flow movements or changes in the viscosity of the gels during the settling phase of opal formation. Another typical feature of natural opal that is easily duplicated is the formation of rather mosaic patterns through the beds of settled spheres. In side elevation, these arrays are parallel columns. Sections cut horizontally through specimens show a checkerboard effect. Spheres settling in synthetic systems naturally take up positions in such geometrical arrays of "domains" and the ultimate effect may be compared with a layer of parallel columnar crystals interlocking with one another in the horizontal plane. A suitably placed cross-section gives a "harlequin" effect.

The foregoing requirements for the natural

**Plate 67:** Rough opal from Yowah, Queensland.

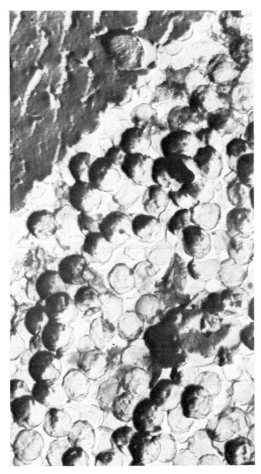

**Figure A:** × 25,000 Silica particles naturally formed in opal from Coober Pedy.

**Figure B:** × 25,000 Synthetic particles of silica made in CSIRO laboratories. (For comparison with Figure A.)

**Plate 68:** A cut stone of Queensland boulder opal.

**Plate 69:** (*overleaf*) Four different positions of the same opal. This "solid", from Lightning Ridge, illustrates the play of colours which many opals exhibit as they are turned.

deposition of precious opal rather than the common varieties are so restrictive that it is not surprising to find that good gem material is rare. There are, however, even further obstacles to the formation of the gemstone, especially those arising in the course of cementation of the settled arrays of spheres. As first formed, the beds of spheres are soft and deformable. A period of gradual drying must eventually occur if the mass is to be hardened by deposition of further silica from solution both within and between the spheres. This "silicification" can give both mechanical strength and a degree of optical transparency to the mass. If it does not proceed far enough, the stone can be of too high a water content to be stable when mined and brought out into dry air, and such material will craze, split and become opaque. If it proceeds too far, the stone can become clear, hard and glassy and the regularly arranged optical discontinuities responsible for the fire may be removed. Some clear "jelly" opals and Mexican opals show faint, diffuse fire effects that correspond to a stage of almost complete elimination of diffracting discontinuities through advanced silicification. The technique of achieving a useful degree of hardening, without ruining the fire, is the most difficult part of synthetic opal preparation and indeed is still far from being perfected to the stage where the material could withstand normal conditions of wear that apply to the natural stone.

In conclusion, we should perhaps comment on two of the issues now most frequently being raised; first, whether our work could help locate opal occurrences; and second, whether synthetic opal is likely to become competitive with the natural stone. We believe that localities for precious opal must be more common and wide-spread in western NSW, southern Queensland and the northern parts of South Australia than has been realised. In these arid areas, wherever horizontal beds of bentonitic clays, such as those in the Cretaceous sequence, occur within 100 feet of the surface opal could be expected near the junctions of such beds with overlying porous sandstones. The search could well concentrate on locating ground-water traps of this type at shallow depth. One of the greatest barriers to exploration is the extent to which such formations are covered by a surface layer of extremely hard "silcrete", otherwise called "duricrust" or "grey-billy", in such regions. The presence of this material does not indicate that the rocks immediately beneath were not porous enough to permit evaporation and opal deposition in recent geological times, since it is a late-stage deposit and can be subsequent to a period of opal formation. As a sheer mechanical barrier to a search it is, however, most formidable.

Finally, regarding the future of synthetic opal, we are not convinced that it could ever be produced in a form indistinguishable from natural opal, therefore we would expect that the situation might become, eventually, the same as that which applies to the supply of other synthetic gems. As long as the natural stones can be identified, there is no real competition from the synthetics, which tend to become established as separate entities in their own distinct markets. Although years of progressive development of methods for preparing synthetic opal may ultimately lead to an attractive and practical decorative material, the natural stone has certain special features that reflect its formation over a great period of time. We believe that these will not be reproducible in synthetics and even if electron microscope replica techniques have to be used, distinctions between natural and synthetic opals will be preserved.

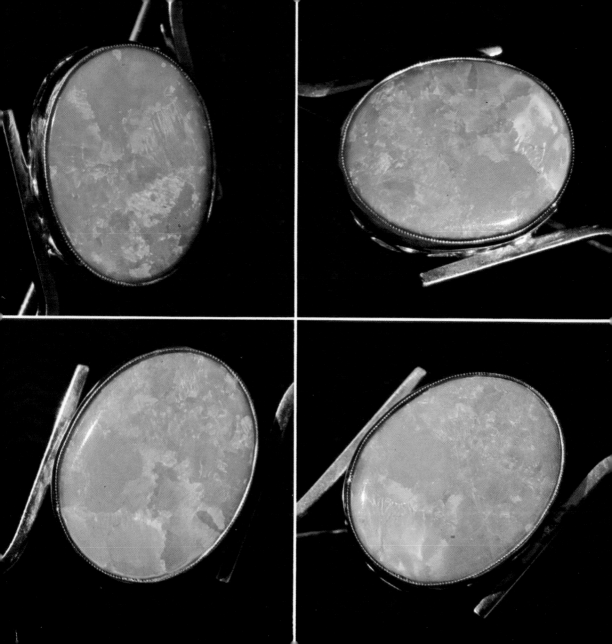

# HOW TO CUT OPAL

THERE are many ways of cutting opal. Old timers on the fields will swear by their time-honoured methods. Cutters who use more modern abrasives and polishing powders will treat the old-timers' methods with smiling tolerance. It must be admitted that today's standards require that many field-cut stones, especially from Lightning Ridge, must be recut or repolished before being set in jewellery.

*Machinery required*
1. Grinding machine, for cleaning and shaping the rough stone.
2. Rotary, horizontal lapping plate—sometimes with curved grooves.
3. Sanding discs.
4. Polishing wheel.

Opals can be cut, ground and polished using silicon carbide or aluminium oxide hand stones, and jeweller's rouge on felt. This method however is long and tedious, and is not recommended.

Power tools are usually used, but electricity from a central source is not available on some opal fields. In Coober Pedy there are some privately-owned generators. At Lightning Ridge rural electricity is connected to the immediate township only.

Cutters therefore who do not have a generator use hand-turned grinding machines, or improvise with an oldfashioned treadle sewing machine using foot-power to turn their wheels.

Those miners who have electric power use electric motors (invariably secondhand), of varying capacity, dependent on the type of generator available.

*To cut a one-sided solid opal cabochon*
Carefully examine your piece of opal before you commence cutting. Note where the best colour lies. This will influence your choice for the front. Also note that if the colour occurs in bars, you must orient your stone so that the colour bars are run straight, not askew.

Look for any potch bands, bars or clouds, any cracks or chips, and spots of sand. Flaws will spoil a good stone. Unhappily, quite often potch or sand does not reveal itself until the cutting of stone is nearly completed. It is therefore a wise precaution to examine the stone (wet) with a hand lens under a strong light frequently during each operation.

After choosing the front and deciding how best

A lapidary examines an opal he is cutting.

92

**Plate 70:** Opal pendants in heavy gold settings.

**Plate 71:** Modern brooch and ring settings for opal jewellery.

Making a flat surface on a horizontal lap

to cut, with sufficient cold water playing on your grinding wheels, remove flaws and excess potch from the opal. Do not "work" the opal for extended periods on the wheel, as it will heat up very quickly, and excessive heat will crack it.

Now carefully grind a flat face on the area selected to be the back of your stone. Take into consideration the amount of colour available, depth of stone, and freedom from blemishes, and make this flat face on the back as large as possible. When the back face is finished select a shape on your template which best covers your available colour. Now, with an aluminium or lead pencil (sharply pointed) accurately outline the template shape on the back of your opal.

Grind the excess edges away evenly, to just outside your pencil mark. Grind a bevel on the back. The opal is now ready to be dopped. Select

a dop with a head of a size to fit *within* the outline of your stone, and prepare to dop on this pencilled side. We use metal dopsticks, made from aluminium roofing nails, with the heads from 5 mm to 12 mm in diameter.

Dopping opal can be a tricky business, as the stone must *not* be exposed to sudden or excess heat. Long, low heating under a reading-lamp before dopping is a good safety precaution.

A dopping mixture of sealing wax and shellac put through a mincer to break it into granules, is stored in a small open container. Have this close to hand.

Light your spirit lamp, and, holding a metal dopstick firmly (by the end away from the head) in tweezers or pliers, heat the shank in the flame. Hold the nail upright after each heating, and allow the heat to travel up towards the head of

**Plate 72:** Andamooka opal which has been flattened on a horizontal lap in preparation for doublet-making.

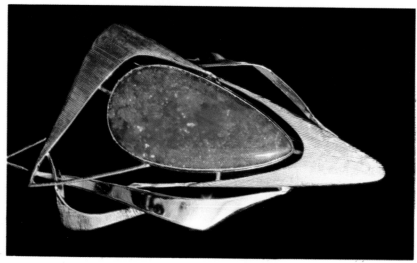

**Plate 73:** Sculptured gold setting for an opal brooch.

Opals on wooden dop sticks.

the nail. Now dip the nail-head briefly into the dopping-wax granules and allow the wax to melt, having heated your opal separately before dopping, perhaps under an incandescent globe in a reading-lamp.

Experience will tell you the exact second to put the head of the nail (now covered in molten wax) on to your warmed opal. When you do this immediately lift the nail to a vertical position. Your opal should now be lightly attached to the dop head. Heat will continue to travel upwards and so securely attach it to the dop head. Lightly rewarm the *body* of the nail, *not* the opal.

Stand your opal on its dopstick upright in a holder, and allow it to cool. Particular swiftness of handling, and extra care, need to be exercised when dopping doublets which have been attached with shellac.

To remove the opal from the dopstick, place it for several minutes in the refrigerator, or gently heat the body of the metal dopstick in the flame of the spirit lamp (remove the opal carefully with the fingers). Re-dop the opal to sand and polish the back (if required). Remove the opal from the dop as before, and clean with a soft cloth lightly damped with methylated spirits.

*Points to Remember when Cutting Opal*

Opal needs a light touch. It is a soft, brittle material (hardness $5\frac{1}{2}$–$6\frac{1}{2}$ on Mohs' scale) and sudden or over-heating will cause cracks to appear.

Always wet the opal to examine the colour. Hold it up to a strong light or sunlight to see whether any sand, cracks, or impurities are hidden which could cause disappointment in the finished stone.

If the opal shows solid colour the stone may be cut to a "solid" stone (which will carry most value). Or the opal may be sliced to provide thin colour bands to be made later into doublets. If an opal doublet is faced with a thin cover of protective crystal it is known as a triplet.

The extent of the colour will decide the shape of the stone. Formal shapes are most popular,

**Plate 74:** Opals for doublet making: Note the template outlines.

STAGES IN CUTTING AND POLISHING OPALS

1. Excess material is cut away by a thin diamond saw from an opal doublet.

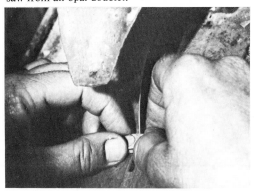

2. The shape is refined on a diamond wheel.

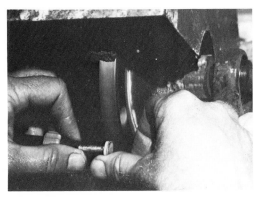

but beautiful freeform pieces are often dictated by the flow of colour markings in the stone.

Opals may be cut into either single cabochons or double-sided cabochons, in high or low form.

Never use excessive pressure on opal, especially on the grinding wheels. Do not work for more than a few seconds at a time on the wheels. Inspect your work closely and constantly.

A slitting saw may be used to cut the opal into slabs or to cut between the colour bands.

Do not hesitate in experimenting with your hand movements to achieve the technique of shaping, but examine your work often. Sometimes the lightest touch on the wheel will be all that is necessary to remove a small amount of the stone in order to achieve symetry. Remember in all your work on opal—one quarter of your time will be spent on working on the stone, and three-quarters of your time will be spent in examining the work.

It must be remembered that because of the soft nature of opal, a certain amount of the stone will be lost on the sanding and pumice wheels. Allowance must be made for this loss when the stone is being ground to shape. In other words, do not take the stone down too far on the grinder.

Examine the opal cabochon carefully to avoid "flats".

After each operation on the wheels wash the hands, dopstick and stone.

It is a matter of personal preference, together with the extent of the best presentation of colour in your opal, whether you increase the angle of the dome of the front of the stone. In order to do this you must remember to place the girdle slightly more towards the back of the stone when you are grinding the initial shape of the back.

After polishing wipe the finished stone carefully with a tissue lightly dampened with methylated spirits. This will remove any adhering dopping wax.

Plate 75: "Solids" cut from opal mined at Coober Pedy, S.A.

Plate 76: Opal doublets in hard-gold-plated sterling silver mounts, before the "claws" have been burnished over.

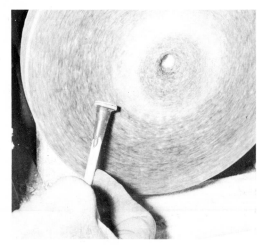

Pre-polishing process on pumice wheel.

4. The opal is polished on a leather lap wet down with cerium oxide in methylated spirits.

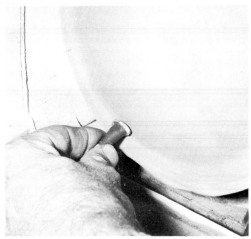

Taking scratches out on the sanding disc.

**Plate 77:** A display of brightly-coloured opal doublets.

# OPAL DOUBLETS

SO MUCH OPAL comes in thin seams and in broken pieces of skin shells, that doublets have been evolved in order to make the material "go further", and to give a greater depth and brilliancy to pale "jelly" and even "grey" opal, for jewellery manufacture.

Opal doublets are *never* intended to deceive. Natural doublets occur, especially at Lightning Ridge, and can be extremely valuable. Most black opal occurs in this way—a thin band of brilliance on a background of black potch.

It is only when opal doublets are set in jewellery, and the junction between opal and the backing is covered, that unscrupulous merchants can label them "genuine solid black opal", when they are nothing of the sort.

A little practice will enable anyone to immediately recognise an opal doublet. The gemstone is usually flat, or with a very slight dome. High-domed, over-bright stones with a distinct line at the girdle, will be triplets. Doublets will have a distinct, straight black line at the girdle, separating the two pieces (this is the lamp black, or black pencil used to darken the backing). If black potch has been used as a backing, the exercise will be a little more difficult. If white or grey potch, black or red glass, porcelain or chalcedony have been used, the junction will be easily distinguished.

*To Make an Opal Doublet*

Take a piece of potch and flatten it to perfection on a rotary lap. Andamooka "jelly" makes the brightest doublets. Grind away the flaws from your piece of jelly opal, and flatten it to perfection on the lap—use the best and brightest side of your piece. *This is important*, for the side you have selected will eventually become the front of your stone.

Two methods of cementing the potch and the opal together are used:
1. With shellac. Both flat sides are first darkened with black pencil.
2. With epoxy resin, mixed with lamp black.

Join the two *flat* pieces together. If an epoxy resin is used, the stone must be allowed twenty-four hours to set. Stones which have been joined with shellac may be worked as soon as they are cool.

When the joint has set grind off all the excess potch. Trim the sides of the stone to show the characteristic thin line at the girdle. Grind the back to the desired thickness (about 3 mm). Shape the front until the colour shows bright and clear.

*Methods*
1. Shape on grinders 100 and 220.
   Sand on 400 cloth, 600 cloth.
   Use coarse pumice wheel.
   Polish on Linde A, tin oxide or rouge on leather.
2. As above, but substitute paper for cloth sanding-discs.
3. Shape stone on 100 and 220 silicon carbide grinding wheels.
   Sand on 600 cloth.
   Pre-polish on pumice.
   Polish on cerium oxide in water.
4. Shape stone on 100 and 220 silicon carbide wheels.
   Sand on 400 and 600 cloth discs.
   Polish on domed leather buff, dampened with cerium oxide in methylated spirits.
5. Shape stone on 100 silicon carbide grinding wheel.

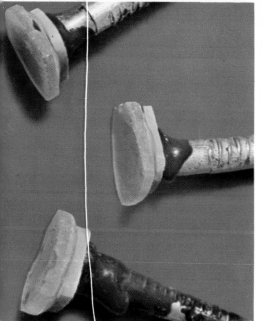

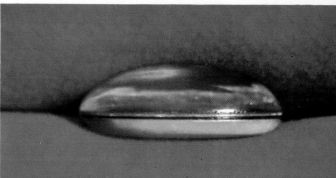

**Plate 78:** (A) Slices of clear quartz, used for making opal triplets. Note the typical faces of the six-sided hexagonal crystal system to which quartz belongs. (B) Precision cut and polished triplets tops in clear quartz, mass produced in accurate millimetre sizes to "standard" jewellery shapes. (C) Triplets in the making. Cemented potch, precious opal and slices of clear quartz are attached to dop-sticks, ready for the next stage of being shaped on the grinding wheels. (D) Side view of an opal triplet. This clearly shows: the common opal base of the stone; the girdle (showing back pigment under the thin wafer of precious opal; clear quartz top.

Refine shape on 220 metal bonded diamond wheel.

Sand on 600 silicon carbide cloth.

Pre-polish on 300/400 micron diamond powder on nylon cloth then on 6–12 micron diamond powder on nylon cloth.

Polish on domed leather, splashed with cerium oxide in methylated spirits.

## OPAL TRIPLETS

AN OPAL TRIPLET is a three-piece stone, manufactured by cementing together a backing piece, a thin slide of precious opal, and a thin layer of crystal quartz so that one complete stone results.

The quartz tops may be obtained by slicing through a crystal of quartz, as in Plate 78A, or by the purchase of precision-cut and polished triplet tops.

Firstly, a flat, thin piece of precious opal is cemented on to a backing of common opal, glass or porcelain, which has been first darkened as described for opal doublets.

The surface of the precious opal does not require to be sanded and polished.

The quartz top is then cemented to the precious opal with a clear resin (preferably a single component adhesive which does not require any mixing, such as a cyano-acrylate type). Bubbles are difficult to exclude from two-component adhesives when they are mixed, and their presence detracts from the pure clarity of a finished stone.

When the pre-cut quartz tops are used, there is no more work to be done, apart from finishing off the backs of the triplets.

When slices of quartz are used, the stones must be shaped, ground, sanded and polished in the same manner as for solids and doublets.

Low domes are used on the smaller stones, but high quartz domes are usually placed on triplets larger than 12 × 10 mm.

The better the quality of the opal used for triplets, the brighter will be the stone. Andamooka jelly is very suitable.

The quartz tops do double duty. They protect the opal, which is less hard than the quartz, and they scatter and enhance the colours of the opal.

As a rule, opal triplets are more expensive to buy than opal doublets.

To distinguish a triplet from a solid stone, if set in jewellery, hold the piece in a horizontal position, and look through the dome. If the opal is a solid, the colour will be evident; if the stone is a triplet, the colourless quartz top only will be seen.

A word of warning: Manufacturers in the orient have recently evolved a process of making "opal" triplets which contain no opal at all. These "schnapper-skin" triplets are made by using a **layer of fish skin instead of opal, red or blue dye** being mixed with the cementing agent.

"Schnapper skin" triplets are very difficult to detect, especially if they are set into a piece of jewellery, but under examination with a hand lens, the fish skin at the girdle shows as grey, with a layer of dye behind it.

They can easily deceive anyone who is not an expert in identifying opal, and are a positive threat to people who think they are buying a triplet made with genuine Australian opal. Although to the untrained eye they look exactly like opal, the colours (especially the reds) are false hues, and are flat, without depth, when compared with the vibrant colours of the natural stone.

**Plates 79, 80:** Opal triplets.

# PROCESS FOR TREATING MATRIX OPAL

THE PROCESS is applied to finished stones because with some matrix material the penetration of colour is so small that polishing the stone would remove the dyed layer.

Most opal matrix, found at Andamooka, is a pale, porous, and chalky substance, with flashes of colour in streaks. This material can be stained to give a dark body colour, against which the opal colours appear quite brilliant. This type of stone does not carry the value of opal. Some stones cut from the opal matrix are given a covering of clear quartz.

Not all matrix is suitable for dyeing, and material should be chosen after examination with a hand lens. With practice the pattern of material suitable for dyeing can be recognised, but if in doubt—try it. Any material with large pores or shaley areas should be discarded as these will finish as black blobs.

The process consists of three operations:

1. Opal matrix is immersed in a strong sugar-water solution for a period of a few hours to three or four days depending on the porosity. Penetration by the sugar solution may be accelerated by gently heating the solution. Evaporation losses must be replaced, as a too concentrated solution becomes too viscous to penetrate the pores of the opal. If the equipment is available the specimens may be treated under vacuum. Certain other organic compounds may be used in place of sugar but results to date have shown that sugar gives the blackest result.

2. The specimens then are transferred—without washing—to concentrated sulphuric acid and left soaking for some hours. N.B. *Sulphuric acid is extremely corrosive and should be handled with great care*. It also has a very strong affinity for water, so one always adds acid to water and in small amounts at a time.

3. The specimens are then removed from the acid, allowed to drain and then thoroughly washed in water until all traces of acid have been removed.

The dyeing is now completed, and should the colour be not deep enough the process is repeated until the desired colour is obtained, or material rejected as unsuitable.

The sulphuric acid oxidises the sugar and leaves a fine residue of carbon in the interstices of the opal specimen. It is this layer of carbon which absorbs scattered white light and so enhances the diffracted colour.

Other methods of treatment of opal matrix are employed, which include the chemical deposition of oxides of manganese within the porous structure of the stone. The main advantage of this latter method is that a better penetration can be achieved.

Note: large pieces of natural black opal matrix have also been found at Andamooka. The colours are full of fire, and the stones could easily be mistaken for Lightning Ridge black opal when cut and polished.

# OPAL CHIPS SET IN PLASTIC

A popular method of using opal chips which are too small to make into jewel stones, is to set them in plastic, with a dark background (usually black).

Suitable moulds of polyethylene, glass, or

**Plate 82:** Opal in matrix from Andamooka before cutting and treating.

**Plate 81:** Matrix opal cut, dyed, and mounted.

ceramic are used. Attractive jewellery, ornaments and souvenir items can be made by this method, but use the brightest possible opal chips.

The chips are set in the synthetic resin by a series of comparatively simple processes. Individual methods vary slightly, depending on the type of plastic resin used, and it is essential that the resin manufacturers' directions are followed faithfully. It pays to practise embedment with inferior material first, to observe results, and so profit by experience.

A short summary of the work follows:

1. Select chips for embedment which are free from sand and potch.
2. Obtain a highly polished wax finish on the mould to be used.
3. Use disposable containers to hold the resin; do your work on several thicknesses of paper; do not inhale the fumes.
4. The first layer of plastic is put into the mould and allowed to set.
5. The second layer of plastic is put on top of the first layer. The opal chips are dipped in resin and placed in the second layer. This layer is allowed to become quite hard, before proceeding. The time taken to harden will vary with the temperature.
6. A dark pigment is mixed in the resin and put into the mould as the third and final layer. The work must be left undisturbed at all times. When hard, the article is removed from the mould. Methods of removal will vary, depending on the type of mould used.
7. If the chips are to be set directly into jewellery or on to an article with a solid back, the process is slightly different. The pigment is then contained in the first layer, and the final layer is carefully built up to form a meniscus.

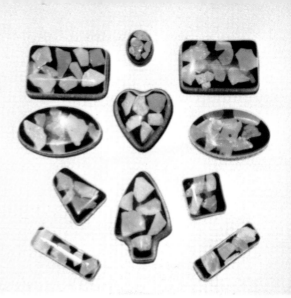

**Plate 83:** Small opal chips as used in the making of opal-chip jewellery and ornaments.

**Plate 84:** Opal chips embedded in a synthetic resin, with a black-pigmented backing.

**Plate 85:** Brooches and pendant of opal chips cast in plastic.

# INDEX

(Plate numbers are in bold type)

**Plate 86:** A collection of opal brooches, styled by a leading jewellery designer. Freeform opals of random shape have been used, in contrast to the widely accepted practice of cutting opal to formal shapes in "standard" sizes.

Opal has risen in price to such an extent in recent years that it is less wasteful of material to "cut to colour", rather than to a pre-planned shape.

# ACKNOWLEDGMENTS

We have enjoyed preparing this book.

Not only were we working with materials which always claim our interest, but we renewed friendships on the opal fields with people for whom we have great respect and admiration.

Our thanks go to the good folk who lent specimens for us to photograph.

We also thank Messrs A. J. Gaskin, P. J. Darragh, and J. V. Sanders of the CSIRO for their permission to reprint their paper entitled "The Nature and Origin of Opal". We extend our thanks to the editorial committee of the *Australian Gemmologist* for their permission to use the above work, which first appeared in this magazine in December 1966.

We also thank the personnel of the Mines Departments in NSW, Queensland, and South Australia for their courtesy and help, and their permission to use material from their publications. Others to whom we are indebted include the editor of the *Cunnamulla Watchman*, the editor of the *Queensland Mining Journal*, and the staff of the South Australian Government Tourist Bureau.

We are privileged to number Messrs Ray Richards, Don Sinclair and John Reed of the House of Reed amongst our special friends, and we take this opportunity to express our appreciation for their sound guidance and unfailing encouragement.

NANCE AND RON PERRY